Madhu Tandan lived for seven years in a remote Himalayan monastery where every experience was viewed as an opportunity to grow. Her life there, threaded by her dreams, inspired her first book, *Faith & Fire: A Way Within* (1997). She has since written two more, *Dreams & Beyond: Finding Your Way in the Dark* (2009) and *Hemis: A Novel* (2018), to wide acclaim.

Madhu has conducted dream workshops, written articles on dreams and contributed short stories to anthologies. She has presented papers on religious dreaming at international conferences, including the Nouvelle Sorbonne in Paris, and Wasan Island in Canada. She was awarded a writing fellowship at Hawthornden Castle, Edinburgh.

Her husband and she live in the hills of Sattal with the birds and butterflies.

THE LOGIC OF DREAMS

Madhu Tandan

SPEAKING
TIGER

SPEAKING TIGER BOOKS LLP
125A, Ground Floor, Shahpur Jat, near Asiad Village,
New Delhi 110049

Published by Speaking Tiger Books 2022

Copyright © Madhu Tandan 2022

ISBN: 978-93-5447-350-0
eISBN: 978-93-5447-355-5

10 9 8 7 6 5 4 3 2 1

Typeset in Adobe Jenson Pro by SÜRYA, New Delhi
Printed at HT Media Ltd, Greater Noida

All rights reserved.
No part of this publication may be reproduced, transmitted,
or stored in a retrieval system, in any form or by any means,
electronic, mechanical, photocopying, recording or otherwise,
without the prior permission of the publisher.

This book is sold subject to the condition that it shall not,
by way of trade or otherwise, be lent, resold, hired out,
or otherwise circulated, without the publisher's prior
consent, in any form of binding or cover other
than that in which it is published.

*To
Ashishda,
the measure of all things.*

*And to
Richa,
for snow in summer.*

CONTENTS

My Dialogue with Dreams: A Personal Introduction   9

1. Down the Rabbit Hole of Dreams   21
2. Oh! But Why Do We Dream?   36
3. What's This Dream Telling Me?   54
4. Why Do We Keep Dreaming the Same Dreams?   71
5. Nightmares: Terrors of the Dreaming World   90
6. Choices, the Hinges of Destiny   96
7. If Love Is the Answer, What May Be the Question?   115
8. Not One Drop of My Self-Worth Depends on Your Acceptance of Me   136
9. The Snake Catches Its Tail: Breakthrough Dreams   154
10. The Sentinels of the Body— Illness and Healing Dreams   174
11. Seriously Strange: The Paranormal Dream   188
12. Dying and Mourning   209
13. Awake and Dreaming—The Lucid Dream   225
14. Self-Enquiry and Dreams: Dreaming in a Himalayan Monastery   245

Acknowledgements   265
Notes   267
Select Bibliography   273

My Dialogue with Dreams:
A Personal Introduction

At the age of eighteen I was fairly confused about what I wanted to do with my life. I then met my teacher, Sri Madhava Ashish (affectionately known as Ashishda), an English aircraft-engineer-turned-Hindu monk, in his remote hermitage in the Himalayan interior. It took a thirty-six-hour journey by bus to a sleepy village in the hills, followed by a forty-five-minute walk up a steep track covered with burnished pine needles, to get there.

In the evening, by the light of an oil lamp in the dark stillness of the mountains, I asked him, 'What should I do with my life? What direction should I take, and how will I know if it's the right one?'

He surprised me by saying, 'If you like, record your dreams. They will tell you what to tackle first.'

'But I don't remember my dreams,' I said.

'You will if you pay attention to them. Keep a notebook next to your bed and jot down whatever you remember in the morning.'

At the time, his suggestion to record dreams did not mean much to me. It seemed a far-fetched idea that those jumbled, disjointed, often weird, nightly visuals could hold a key to knowing about myself. Yet his words were like a stimulant injected imperceptibly into my sleep, for I found myself waking in the morning with vague but persistent memories of dreams, which made me mildly curious about them. A few months later I recalled a dream with absolute clarity because it was so disturbing.

> *We are travelling in a caravan. A car stops in front of us. Two people get out of it. One of them is Annie Besant. She lifts a small girl of about nine or ten, who appears to be dead, out of the car. Suddenly Annie Besant's face changes and begins to look frightening as it enlarges and sags, making her look ninety years old.*

I wrote to Ashishda and he responded promptly: 'The dream probably alludes to an emotional trauma you experienced. I wonder if you know that Annie Besant "adopted" Krishnamurti as her son, to finally groom him to become the successor to the Theosophical Society. The dream is probably centred on the theme of adoption, since it has picked up symbols connected with that topic. When dreams refer to particular numbers, try and look for what their association is for you. Did something happen at the age of nine or ten that felt like a kind of emotional death?'

How could he have known from my dream about a conflict that I had not even fully admitted to myself? He had then asked me to think back on what happened at the age of nine or ten, as though the age of the dead girl in the dream had something to do with me. I later realized that Annie Besant's age was also calling attention by repeating the age of the dead girl (90 = 9 x 10).

Looking back, I know it was neither his suggestion to note my dreams, nor his book-lined study with all the high priests of dream analysis like Freud and Jung rubbing shoulders with each other that had impressed me about him. It was his interpretation of my dream that stunned me. He accurately pinpointed something long buried within me that needed to be confronted. Only I had to agree to do so.

Throughout my twenty years' association with him, I took as many dreams as I could remember to discuss with him. Ever since, dreams have been the compass that have helped me navigate the unmapped terrain of my inner and outer life.

The waking mind may fool itself and blur the distinction between the desirable and the real. The dreaming mind never does so. It never equivocates. It tells the truth as plainly as a mirror. But what is this 'truth' we are talking about?

Five years after our marriage, Rajeev and I were fortunate in establishing a comfortable life for ourselves. We functioned quite normally in our world of work, family and friends. At a more private level, a voice within also laid claim on us, asking questions whose answers eluded us. I was sometimes struck by the purposelessness of much of my activity, how shatteringly prosaic my concerns were. I felt this day-to-day reality I lived in couldn't be all that life is about. But what was the alternative to it? A place surrounded by trees where the clear air soothed the wavy outlines of thought into an even, rhythmic breathing. A quiet space where work and contemplation joined hands to share the secrets of both worlds. A life like Ashishda's, where every experience held the promise of wholeness.

But big changes can only happen when the time

is right, or when there is a turnaround in season. We were far from being like those ancient trees which can effortlessly shed their autumn leaves. In our tree the sap was still green; if we shook it, perhaps not even a single leaf would fall on its own. Rajeev was just past thirty and I past twenty-five. Amidst this dilemma I dreamt:

> *We are in a plane with no seats. A friend and a few other people are there. At a predetermined moment we are all expected to jump out without parachutes. My friend says that it's impossible to take such a high-risk jump without adequate training. While she is speaking, I look out of the plane and see far away in the distance the outlines of people who have already jumped. I realize that they are not falling, but seem to have touched invisible ground in mid-air. Each of them has a look of great happiness.*
>
> *I point them out to my friend and say, 'Look at them. They made the jump although they were untrained. We've got to do it, otherwise this plane will be our home forever.'*
>
> *The hatch at the bottom of the plane opens and we prepare to jump.*

On waking, I wondered whether the jump that needed to be made was a symbolic or a literal one. My hesitation in the dream to make the jump rose from my trepidation at exchanging my comfortable, sedentary city life for the one in Ashishda's Himalayan ashram, where we would have to plant, weed and harvest crops, milk cows and sustain ourselves entirely by our own labour. Being city bred, I was not 'trained' or in any way attuned to this alien, rural lifestyle where the nearest marketplace was one hour by jeep and the basic necessities of life had to be worked for rather than picked off a shelf. The dream was pointing out that though untrained, like myself, the people who had made the jump were happier for it. Six months later, we decided to relocate to Ashishda's ashram. The assurance in the dream was in a way instrumental in helping me make the jump.

After seven years, when Rajeev and I decided to return to the city, what I dreaded most was being away from Ashishda's presence as also the absence of the unique atmosphere of the Himalayas and the environment he had created. It had afforded us the best opportunity for our inner search. Distanced from that, would we lose touch with what we believed to be most essential in life? Would our inner life become submerged in the swamp and mire of city life?

In the transition from the secluded, focused mountain life to the noisy jostle of the city, I dreamt so often of our life in the ashram, of our tiny cottage. It was evident that though I had physically moved away from it, emotionally, I still resided there. Then, many months later, I dreamt:

I'm closing the gate right outside our mountain cottage and I walk down the road without a backward glance.

Maybe it was from this point onwards that I did manage to 'close the gate' on our life in the mountains, and without a 'backward glance' made an important emotional shift to my new life. But I knew that a great deal more had to be tackled before the transition was complete. The power of our years in the ashram lay in the complexity of our experience there. In order to understand my experiences better, I began to write, trying to maintain some chronological order, of what Ashishda had taught us. I did not quite realize what I was going through at the time, but once again my dream apparently did:

> *There is a house under construction, which has a basic wall, a rudimentary roof, and no floor. Construction material—sand, cement, rubble—is lying all around as I enter this structure. The only furniture inside is an old table on which my typewriter rests. I begin typing from the notes I had made the previous day.*
>
> *A woman wearing stiletto heels enters. She has long, painted fingernails, perfectly groomed hair, and rather fancy clothes. As she moves towards me her high heels wobble on the uneven floor. Her carefully modulated voice, her expensive clothes, her made-up face do not sit comfortably in this rough environment. I get up and after a few polite words usher her out. I then take the typewriter from the table and set it down on the ground.*

It seemed a strange dream! The typewriter gave me the initial clue that the dream was centred on my writing. The house under construction was a symbol alluding to my manuscript. It was, as described by the dream, at a very rudimentary stage—the 'structure' of the story was still very basic. There was construction material lying around, indicating that the material for the book was available, but I still had to give it form. Prompted by that well-groomed woman in the dream, whose presence I found incongruous in that setting, I looked for what was manicured or superficial in my current draft. Once more, the clue lay in the typewriter: I pick it up from the table and place it on the floor. The dream was urging me to *ground* my writings, to base them on my own experiences.

So far, my draft was only a record of incidents and teachings, as though I was not a participant but merely a scribe noting events without daring personal involvement. As a result, it was out of touch with my own feelings.

I heeded my dream advice and began rewriting.

I am not suggesting that every time I had a problem a dream would miraculously give me the solution. There were a number of long stretches when I could not remember any dream, and there were times when they seemed to say nothing about what I thought was important. It would seem as though my dream life had simply gone to sleep. But I do not think that was really the case. My dream life was just marking time till the intensity of the problem had built up sufficiently for its insights to be ingested. Then, it would come, to appease the hunger of my waiting.

Perhaps the dreaming mind's most powerful yet inscrutable face is its metaphysical one, which asks questions whose answers seem to go far beyond the inner and outer life of the individual. I too was confronted with such a disconcerting question.

I was forty by then and had come full circle. Twenty-two years earlier, I had ventured out to discover my path. I had since met a charismatic teacher, under whose vigilant tutelage I had lived for seven years. Another seven had elapsed since our return to the city—time enough to absorb the intense experience of discipleship. But now I was up against an even more fundamental question:

How deep was my commitment to my inner search? It was no longer being shouldered by Ashishda, for he had passed on. I was faced with assuming the responsibility of sustaining my search without any external inputs, for what had been taken for granted when he was alive had to be revivified entirely by my own effort. It raised uncomfortable questions about my dedication. How much did I really want it? How much was I prepared to surrender to it?

I oscillated between holding on to my inner search, and letting my grip loosen. That I often fell short was apparent to me. This dream came against the backdrop of this unarticulated conflict:

> *I'm sitting for an examination, and the invigilator hands me the question paper. I realize this is no ordinary examination—it is a life exam. The first question is: What is your gravest doubt in life?*
>
> *I answer, 'My doubt is that nothing is permanent. Everything changes. Today's pleasure is tomorrow's sorrow; despair turns to hope, health to illness, love to indifference. In this constant flux what is permanent?'*
>
> *I continue to write in this vein for some time, and then feel that I need to get on to the next question, since time is running out. Even though I have not completed my answer, curiosity compels me to turn the page over and look at what the next question is. In rather bold letters it asks: Who are you?*

It was indeed not an ordinary exam. It was a life exam, where my doubts themselves were under scrutiny, an answer being elicited from me in order that I become fully aware of them. The dream was unexpected because

I did not know what my gravest doubts were. Yet, in the dream, my answering the question seemed very normal. If everything changes, where, then, can I find permanence amidst this constant flux? When I turn the page, the next question challenges me by asking, 'Who are you?' making me wonder if the two questions were related to one another. Possibly, the doubts themselves would lead me deeper into this enquiry of one's true nature.

The second question invoked the central teaching of the great South Indian sage Ramana Maharshi who believed the best way to realize the true nature of the Self was through an assiduous enquiry centred on the question: Who am I?

On the face of it, not knowing who one is seems ludicrous. In the days that followed I began to realize how difficult the exercise was. No matter how much I reflected on it, I was confronted with inadequate answers. If I addressed the question by my gender (woman), or my roles (wife, daughter, writer), or by abstract personal qualities (empathetic, introverted, impractical), no satisfactory answers emerged.

It seems that I am something more than my body, more than its desires and fears, more than the mind with all its thoughts and creativity and more than the chain of events I call my life. I may think that the sum of my personality traits, my thoughts and my emotions define the person I am, but in essence that is still not 'me', for when asleep they are not in evidence, yet I still am. Furthermore, my thoughts and emotions constantly change; my body undergoes changes, my personality traits change. How, then, can I search for an answer based on ever-changing attributes? There has to be a permanent 'someone' to whom these changes occur. Who is that 'someone', the unchanging 'I'?

I continue to seek an answer to the question.

~

At one point in time, I felt disadvantaged due to my lack of specialization, even though I majored in psychology and have faithfully kept a record of my dreams for more than forty years. But as I actively engaged with the world of dreaming I realized that what I had considered my handicap was proving to be an advantage. The expert adopts a specialized approach towards dream meanings. The distinct advantage I had was that while taking cognizance of various dream theories, I was not wedded to any particular one. This gave me the freedom to explore the myriad avenues that dreaming traverses, all the while being aware of the underlying assumptions of these diverse theories. Perhaps a pluralistic approach may afford a wider perspective to dreaming. For it is just this multiplicity—the ability of the dream content to evoke more than one interpretation—that weaves richness into the dream tapestry.

In the pages that follow, I explore this multiple evocation—in range and meaning—through the lives of people I met and interviewed in the course of a decade. Their dreams are not representative of a specialized group, but that of ordinary people. It is a known fact that a specialized setting, say of psychoanalysis, evokes dreams congruent to the belief of the analyst. The dreams narrated to me were spontaneous remembrances and were recounted without any obligation, save the desire to share them. And perhaps by analysing them we may learn a little more about our waking behaviour and aspirations, and also further comprehend the world we live in.

Dreams may not have verifiable meanings like that of scientific postulates, which can be tested, but does that empty them of significance? It may need to be clarified that neither the rationalist (who denies meaning to a dream) nor the ones who ascribe meaning to it can boast of concrete proof. The scientifically-oriented person who denounces dreams is making as much of an assumption based on subjective belief as the person who swears to their meaningfulness. I believe the evidence tilts towards the latter point of view, and my bias is evident in this book.

1. Down the Rabbit Hole of Dreams

We enter our dream world perhaps half a million times in the course of our life. For no one is a non-dreamer and it has been scientifically proven that we all dream a minimum of four dreams every night. The natural question that follows then is: Should we cultivate or neglect our dreams? Are they a secret garden or a wasteland? Let us explore this question through a dream, one taken from the public domain.

In a story in the *Kathasaritsagara*—a collection of eclectic tales compiled by Somadeva around 1070 CE—King Vikramaditya saw the painting of a girl and fell in love with her. One night while dreaming of being passionately united with her, he was suddenly woken up by the watchman. Angry, he banished the watchman and, later, narrated his dream to a friend:

> *I crossed the sea and entered a beautiful city full of armed maidens who rushed at me shouting, 'Kill him! Kill him!' Then an ascetic woman came and said to me, 'My son, the man-hating princess Malayavati is coming this way; she makes her maidens kill any man she sees.'*
>
> *The ascetic woman immediately made me wear a woman's attire. Then the princess entered the house*

> with her maidens. I was so startled because she was the same girl I had seen in the painting. Finally I had seen her in flesh and blood. As soon as she saw me, she forgot her hatred of men and was overpowered by desire, even though I was dressed like a woman. She took me back to her palace, and we played at being married. I then told her who I really was and embraced her, and she reciprocated.

Rather than consider his dream to be a wishful fantasy, the king was convinced that Malayavati existed. After all, he had first seen her in a painting and then in a dream. Hopelessly in love with her, he had confessed to his friend, 'I cannot live without her.'

But how was he to find her? His friend asked the king to draw a map of the city, but no one could recognize the city from the map, until one day a poet visiting from afar was able to.

The poet, oblivious of the king's dream, said to him, 'In that city there dwells a princess named Malayavati who hated men until she saw in a dream a certain man in a monastery. In the dream, she brought him to her palace and married him. But just as she was making love with him, she was awakened by her chambermaid. She fired the maid and vowed to end her life if she did not find that man in the next six months. It has been five months since.'

Rejoicing at the striking resemblance to his own dream, the king immediately set out for the city. On reaching there he heard loud lamentations as the Princess Malayavati was about to self-immolate. King Vikramaditya rushed to the pyre and the princess recognized him. He was exultant with joy and brought his beloved back to his own city.

It seems such a fantastic story: a man and a woman—complete strangers—dream of each other, fall in love, eventually find one another and marry. The enchantment of the story is also by virtue of the shared dream—two unknown people, independently, have the same dream about the other, with a similar end and both dreamers are awoken in an identical manner. The miraculous ending is as unbelievable and unreal as a dream appears on awakening. One wonders therefore whether this was an actual dream or merely a literary device used by the author!

Possibly the theme of two people falling in love because of a dream is universal—King Arthur and Kipling's *Brushwood Boy* being a few examples. When young, the Brushwood boy had often dreamed about a girl in a place next to the sea where they rode together. He is woken up by a policeman called Day. Much later he met this woman but, unlike Malayavati, she didn't recognize him. It was only when they go riding together and he mentions his dream in all its details that she bursts into tears and confesses that she had had the same dream and cries out, 'Then you're the Boy—my Brushwood Boy, and I've known you all my life!' Another author employing the fascination of the shared dream!

In *Anna Karenina*, Tolstoy uses the motif of the shared dream to highlight the bond between Vronsky and Anna. Both had dreamt of a French-speaking peasant, a small and dreadful figure, stooped over and fumbling. After Anna conceives—and before she leaves her husband—she tells Vronsky that she will die because she had had a dream. Vronsky immediately recalls the peasant of his own dream. Their participation in a shared nightmare perhaps foreshadows their eventual fate.

Perhaps lovers meeting in a dream and then actually uniting in waking life is not just a literary device. The narrative is not merely expressing fantasy through a dream. It possibly mirrors a substratum that exists in all of us. Psychoanalysis, of course, would locate this within the unconscious and would contend that it is not just the incredible or phantasmagorical that has been represented in the dream but that which has been repressed. These repressed and forgotten experiences, unable to find expression in their actual form, disguise themselves and appear as the incredible in dreams. The above story could then be understood as an unfulfilled wish of King Vikramaditya which was disguised by his dream. But a niggle remains: Did princess Malayavati have the same wish which was then disguised by *her* dream in a similar manner?

We know how the ancient world would read a prophecy into every dream, and conjecture that these dreams were in fact foretelling the kings or queens, the princes or princesses about their future spouses. Somehow, I feel we will not do justice to the shared dream through the archaic interpretation. Nor will we do so by situating it on the landscape of our psychological reality. In either case we would be loading them in a single direction.

Instead, may we not say that dreams—besides being prophetic or a mirror of the personality—are also full of the mysterious, are enchanting, and may even have a functional element intertwined in them? At one level, they are bizarre and baffling, and yet at another level, their mystery is within our grasp in diverse ways.

It has long been accepted that the waking world

influences the dream world, but in Vikramaditya and Malayavati's story the dream world penetrates into and alters waking reality, thus reversing our beliefs. What is also significant in these stories is that the boundary between dreaming and waking, the ordinary and the miraculous, is porous; there is no segregation between the two states of experience, affirming a seamless interface between them.

Another incredible element is that the man-hater Malayavati miraculously forgets her hatred and reciprocates Vikramaditya's love. Not only that, on the king's confession of his deception of impersonating a woman, she does not feel cheated but responds to his passion with equal ardour.

It seems these dreams are expressing urges present in all of us: the yearning to find the perfect mate, to defy rationality in the face of love. These certainly do not belong to the realm of fantasy even though their realization often borders on the miraculous! But may we not say that Vikramaditya and Malayavati's dreams no longer remain in a lonely, private world and instead, like all shared dreams, 'corroborate one another, fitting together like the pieces of a puzzle and they become verifiable like the waking world'?[1]

Buddhism too places particular importance on dreams in which the same message is relayed to different people on the same night. The Buddha's father, aunt and wife 'shared' the same dream on the night of his departure from home. Three different people had dreams predicting his departure; this was enough to herald the first step in his journey of becoming a world saviour.

Personally, I can attest to the power of the shared dream. One morning, my husband casually mentioned that he had dreamt of a friend, who lived in Mumbai, looking very depressed. I was extremely surprised since I had had a similar dream—of the same friend in the same kind of mood. Without trying to interpret either dream, I called this friend only to learn that the previous night he had got news of his father's death. An ordinary dream assumed a different tenor by virtue of it being a shared dream.

Not only the shared dream, but other kinds of dreams can be equally mysterious and enchanting. That perhaps is the reason all known cultures have delved into dreams and their meanings. Indeed the record of human beings puzzling over them goes back at least five thousand years to the clay tablets of Mesopotamia. Intrigued by these strange, evanescent images people have for long sought to crack the facade of their unintelligibility and fathom their significance.

Dreams seem to be about our concerns but they do not have the orderliness of waking life. The ancient world believed their unintelligibility contained a message from the gods, perhaps a promise or warning. Thus, special attention was accorded to the dreams of kings and high priests for the belief existed that the gods were more likely to appear to the highest among the humans. Presumably, however, it was not long before the ancient world realized that all dreams did not have a message or a prognostication. For in Homer's *Odyssey*, we find the cautious Penelope saying, 'Dreams are awkward and confusing things.' Some come true and some don't. She goes on to postulate that there are two kinds of gates—made of horn and ivory—through which dreams come. Those from the gate of horn will come true while those from the ivory gate will cheat us.

Soon two types of true dreams were recognized, those that foretold directly what would happen, and those that were indirect prognostications clothed in symbols. Perhaps Calpurnia's dream about the murder of Caesar in the Senate was an example of the former type. The dream of Alexander the Great after he had laid siege to the city of Tyre exemplifies the second kind: 'A satyr appeared to him at a distance, and sported with him, but when he endeavoured to catch him, ran away, and that, at length, after much trouble, he caught him.'

His dream interpreter unlocked the symbol by breaking the Greek word for satyr—*satyros*—into '*sa*' and '*tyros*', meaning: Tyre is thine. Alexander had contemplated lifting the siege and returning home, but now, encouraged by his dream, he intensified his efforts and captured the city.

Aristotle refuted the notion that dreams were sent by the gods. He argued that the gods would send them only to people who could make use of them. But dreams came to everybody. Since people did not always make use of them, they could not have originated from the gods. By this reasoning, Aristotle reduced dreams to an activity of the senses, for dreams incorporate bodily sensations experienced when asleep that are transformed into intense dream images. Hippocrates, the father of modern medicine, also came to a similar conclusion, and used dreams to diagnose ailments in his patients. This aspect of dreaming is discussed later in the book.

As dream theories became more complex, a key was developed to interpret dreams. For example, a butterfly sitting on the ring finger would presage the death of the fiancé. Why? Because a caterpillar dies to become a butterfly; likewise, the fiancé (represented by the ring finger) would proceed to the next life. Sometimes it was not the literal content in the dream that would come to pass but its very opposite. The *Brahmavaivarta Mahapurana* reads, 'The one who enjoys the pleasure of the company of an unchaste woman, he achieves a good wife.'[2] Often there was no obvious connection between the dream content and the prediction based on it, save only a pun or a play on words. For example, for the Egyptians, dreaming of buttocks signified that the dreamer's parents would die—the word for buttocks closely resembling that for orphan in their language.

The Christians reversed this position to that of earlier times—dreams were messages from God but only for his elect. The word of God had been given to the Church through the Pope, and people had no need to speak directly to God through dreams. Any further communication outside the ambit of the Church was not encouraged. The dream gradually sank to the level of superstition and was left to gypsies and fortune-tellers.

This Christian discrediting of dreams successfully managed to diminish the value of dreaming in the European world. Whatever residual meaningfulness of dreams may have survived was robbed of them by the emergence of Cartesian dualism—a concept which stated that the world comprises of two distinct and incompatible substances, mind and matter—in the seventeenth century. Dreaming was consigned to the realm of fantasy, hallucination and irrational experience; dreams were deemed a wasteland.

No fresh input stimulated our understanding of dreams; the old notions had run their course and now the subject fell into disrepute, discredited by a growing belief in science. And maybe we, today, have in some way inherited the vestiges of that bias against dreams. We had to wait till the twentieth century and for Sigmund Freud (1856–1939) to provide the next clue to solving the enigma of dreams.

Freud attributed a decisive role to the unconscious in dreams, as also in our lives. The unconscious, he believed, is the repository of unresolved conflicts, traumatic events, forgotten experiences of childhood, as also innate instinctual urges that never became conscious. All these are restrained from expression. However, during the night, the memory of recent experiences (*day residue*) instigates the ungratified wishes buried in the unconscious to seek fulfilment. They threaten to invade our consciousness, but are denied entry by the *censor*—compared by Freud to the censorship employed by repressive regimes as opposed to the freedom of the press—as they may disrupt sleep. The only way wishes can get past the censor is by disguising their content, which we then experience as dream images. This, very briefly, is Freud's disguise-censorship theory. Contrary to the common belief that dreams disturb sleep, Freud perceived them as the guardians of sleep.

More importantly, for him, the dream became a purveyor of our psychological reality. He thus gave birth to the idea that dreams are not a wasteland but a secret garden of the personality. The current dominant Western model, for example, sees the dream as a reflection of our wishes, desires, concerns and aspirations—a mirror of the personality.

However, the psychological model does not exhaustively

define the dream. It allows no conceptual space for a variety of dream types: problem solving, precognition of events and illness, telepathic and shared dreams. The main bulk of dreaming consists of 'ordinary' or 'little' dreams—relatively short episodes that feature strange elements which appear to be based on the manipulation and recombination of memories. But there are also 'extraordinary' or 'big' dreams that linger in consciousness, demanding to be understood. Standing apart from all these types is the lucid dream, where the dreamer is actually aware of being in the dream state.

Part of the fascination of dreams resides in their ability to reveal different facets of our lives—our mind, body, feelings—and, at times, to offer intimations of something even beyond them.

I am going to quote a dream from my files to exemplify this. My neighbour, in her mid-forties, lives with her husband and in-laws. Her marriage, for the most part, is an indifferent one. Now that her daughter is married and well settled, she divides her time between walks and yoga in the mornings and visits in the evenings to her ageing parents who live in an adjacent neighbourhood. When she had this dream, her father was suffering from a malfunctioning prostate and was hospitalized. She dreamt:

> *My husband is bringing my father out of the hospital. My dad has just been discharged and they are both standing outside the hospital building. An old black Fiat drives up and my father's deceased brother emerges from it. My uncle is looking much younger; in fact, he is looking in his prime. He asks my father to sit in the front seat and they drive off. I find myself*

sitting in the back seat and I soon realize that my uncle has come to take my father away. I feel a sense of finality to this act. In desperation, I try and phone my husband to tell him that Dad will not be coming back. I watch them as they drive into an underpass.

At first glance this dream certainly substantiates the belief that dreams replay the events of the past day—her father had been hospitalized and subsequently discharged, and the dream had depicted this with some embellishment. But it could also be a reflection of my neighbour's anxiety about her father's health, an infiltration of the remains of her day (Freud's *day residue*) where, unsupported, she feels trapped between the desire to help her parents and the need to fulfil her obligations towards her marital home. The dream portrays her loneliness, vulnerability and her impotence. Her husband, even though present after the father's discharge, just stands there and makes no effort to escort him home. This is left to her and a dead uncle. Since dead people may not be of much use in assisting someone home, the responsibility, effectively, is only hers. The dream bluntly voices her apprehension—will she be able to cope with looking after her parents in their fading years?

Another view would not treat this as an anxiety dream, but would hold that it presents an inversion of her actual relationship with her father and thereby supports her self-image of a mature individual. Perhaps she had never emerged from the awe in which she held her father as a child. The dream, after all, is about dependence and assistance, portraying an ailing parent and a daughter's desire to help him. It has displaced her sense of dependence on her father and projected it onto his weak health, consequently portraying *him* as the dependent figure. This neatly reverses the roles and now she is the caretaker—the stronger, superior one. The only way she can maintain this superiority in the face of an unequal relationship with her father is to portray him in her dream as passive and helpless.

Or is the dream about the malaise in her marriage—the larger-than-life image she has of her father which is affecting her relationship with her husband? The husband, escorting the father out of the hospital, signifies that he is instrumental in bringing to the surface this fixation on her father. This issue has remained dormant (dead) in their marriage as portrayed by the dead uncle who has come to take him away. She finds herself in the family car with the husband conveniently forgotten. Also, it seems that she drives her marriage from the backseat as seen by her position in the car. She attempts to assure the husband by telling him over the phone that the father will not come back (between them). The father and uncle go underground—the underpass—indicating that the 'sick' father fixation is being buried once again. Viewed thus, the dream appears to be commenting on the 'sickness' within her marriage, her father fixation being the root cause.

These are just three of the many psychological interpretations one could give to the dream. Those inclined towards such a psychological reading will, no doubt, be able to detect the different theories supporting these interpretations. However, there can be a totally different rendering of this dream. It could be anticipating the imminent death of the father. He will come out of the hospital, but may succumb to unforeseen complications soon afterwards. A messenger from the world of death—her deceased uncle—has come to assist him in the crossing, which is depicted in the dream by his departing with the brother. But her attachment propels her into the backseat of the car. This, however, can only be for a very short distance, after which she can only be a mere spectator from her world as they cross over into the *other* world (a vehicular underpass takes you to the other side). Her desperate bid to phone her husband is perhaps reflective of the shock surrounding the death of the father—'Dad will not be coming back.' This interpretation, of course, nudges us into a dimension altogether different from the psychological paradigm of dreams. The dream becomes a premonition.

Perhaps one meaning does not exclude the other. Every one of the interpretations may be relevant to her life situation. Her dream could be a comment on her current anxiety, her seeming impotence in front of the father and the estrangement in her marriage, and could also be anticipating an actual event. In other words, the appropriateness of the psychological interpretations need not preclude the paranormal meaning of the dream. In fact, the dream had other paranormal elements as well, as I was soon to learn.

Curiously, three weeks after my neighbour had recounted her dream to me, as we were walking together one morning, she reminded me of her dream and said, 'Little did I realize that the dream was foretelling my father's death. Nothing in his condition had been that alarming. Neither had the doctors any inkling that he would go so suddenly.' After being discharged her father had developed one complication after another, and had died a week later.

I thought it was her way of telling me that my psychological rendering of her dream was not a correct assessment. 'I am so sorry to learn about your father...' I commiserated.

She began telling me about the funeral, describing the calm expression on her father's face just prior to the cremation. Then she paused and said, 'My husband said that when they were dressing the body it smelt of cigars...like the residual smell after a cigar smoker has left the room.'

'That's odd,' I replied. 'Did your father smoke cigars?'

'Not at all! He never smoked.'

My mind struggled for an explanation. Was it a combination of association and imagination that had triggered her husband's olfactory senses to believe he had smelt cigar smoke in the room? Of course, in the Hindu tradition, it would have been sacrilegious for anyone to smoke while the body was being dressed and anointed for the cremation.

Without my voicing them, she addressed my thoughts: 'No one in the room was a cigar smoker. My husband is a down-to-earth, nuts-and-bolts sort who isn't given to flights of fancy.'

We walked on in silence. Suddenly she said, 'My uncle—he was the cigar smoker!'

My rational beliefs wavered. Was she implying that the cigar aroma was a signature of her dead uncle who had come to ensure a safe passage for his brother into the 'other' world, just as her dream had foretold?

More than one person has recounted vivid dreams to me in which they have been 'visited' by a deceased loved one. I could have treated these dreams as merely psychological projections, in which a powerful wish to contact the departed soul metamorphosed into a potent dream of an actual visitation. Such a view, however, denies the potency of the dreamer's experience—perhaps even does violence to it. However, given a broader understanding of dreams, my neighbour's dream could be read as a visitation from her deceased uncle, who had come to warn her of her father's death.

How are we to make sense of these diverse interpretations? In fact, can dreams really be understood? Aren't their multiple meanings a testimony to their essential meaninglessness? Dream theorists counter that this quality of dreams is akin to the arts, where the beauty of a painting is dependent on the multiple meanings it can evoke. The same is true of literary texts, for which multiple interpretations, even contradictory interpretations, of the same text do not render them meaningless, but enrich them further. If we can accept multiple meanings in literature and art, then why not in dreams?

But before we embark on the adventure of exploring the rabbit hole of dreams, I am going to briefly look, in the next chapter, at laboratory evidence about dreaming.

2. Oh! But Why Do We Dream?

People generally believe dreams are meaningless hallucinations. That the medley of images in them do not mean anything. Kings can turn into cabbages, horses can sing, I could fly or turn into a ferocious tiger, all in the matter of a single dream. They may yet have a meaning, but we are unable to comprehend them because they seem so removed from reality.

Most of us thus grow up believing dreams are unimportant, if not irrelevant, to our lives. Some even deny that they regularly dream. And the general perception is that people who are interested in them are, well, perhaps a little strange. Much of the current public image of dreaming is still shaped by misinformation, fears and superstitions rather than by an informed study of the developments in the field.

Fortunately, laboratory findings have set to rest the doubts that lurk in our minds—to begin with, the millennia-old speculation whether we dream or not. In 1953, serendipitously,[1] conclusive experimental evidence established that we undergo two kinds of sleep; each entirely different from the other. There are sudden bursts of rapid eye movements (REM) under closed eyelids in one, as if a game of tennis were in progress. This is the phase of sleeping wherein dreams are experienced. Besides rapid eye movements, other physiological indicators too attest to the fact that we're dreaming, like electrical activity in the brain, irregularity in breathing, increase in the pulse rate and a loosening of the muscles. The other phase of sleep—NREM, or Non-REM, sleep—is marked by the absence of rapid eye movement, and in this phase dreams are not experienced. On the face of it we seem to be peacefully asleep in the REM phase. Our brain, however, is aroused to the point where the EEG (electroencephalogram) activity resembles that of our normal waking state. It is now a scientifically established fact that each one of us—even if some swear they never dream—dreams at least four or five times every night.

During laboratory studies, when awakened after each episode of REM sleep, and asked if they were dreaming, the subjects actually related a dream. In the morning, even people who did not recall having dreamt had to concede they must have, after hearing their own recorded voice!

Not only has the occurrence of dreams been objectively verified, in fact, laboratories have extensively mapped the entire sleeping state of adults and children alike. We may believe that each of us has a distinctive way of sleeping but it seems we negotiate sleep in a similar manner. Besides the two entirely different phases of sleep, REM and NREM, scientists have also distinguished a short period of transition between waking and sleeping, which is called *sleep onset* or the *hypnagogic* state.

It is very difficult to pinpoint the exact instant of sleep onset, but it is said to occur when a stimulus, like a flashing light, fails to elicit a customary response.

Frequently associated with sleep onset is a feeling of floating or falling, which can often terminate abruptly in a jerk, and return us to wakefulness. Such starts generally occur only during the first five minutes of sleep.

Visual perception of objects ceases with the onset of sleep. The eyes begin to drift slowly from side to side, and this slow eye-rolling is another reliable indicator that sleep has commenced. There is a gradual transition in brain activity from the characteristic rhythms of wakefulness to that of NREM sleep. The NREM phase occurs in four distinct stages, which are simply termed Stage 1, Stage 2, Stage 3 and Stage 4. Brain activity during dreaming or REM sleep, of course, is different from any of these four stages of NREM sleep.

What follows sleep onset is the gradual descent into the deepest part of sleep. Within the first fifteen minutes we enter Stage 1 of the NREM phase. Each new stage is announced by its own typical pattern in the EEG, the brain waves becoming slower in each successive stage. After only a few minutes of Stage 1, we enter Stage 2. Several minutes later the much slower brain waves of Stage 3 become apparent. Another ten minutes and the EEG signals that the sleeper has entered Stage 4, or the deepest part of sleep. By then the body is at its most relaxed and brain rhythms are at their slowest. When awoken, if a person takes a few minutes to reach full awareness, it is likely that he or she has been aroused from this stage of NREM sleep. It is also during this stage that young children experience incidents of sleep talking, sleepwalking, night terrors, and bed-wetting.[2]

These stages occur in the first thirty or forty minutes

following sleep onset. Soon, a series of body movements, like turning on one's side, indicates that the sleeper has now started the re-ascent from the NREM phase. After approximately ninety minutes of sleep, the sleeper displays strikingly different physiological characteristics, and the EEG records markedly different brain rhythms. Cerebral blood flow and brain temperature soar to new heights. Despite this, the body remains totally immobile, and only small convulsive muscular twitches manifest on the face and fingertips. Snoring (if any) ceases, and the breathing becomes irregular—very fast, then slow. Under the eyelids, the eyeballs start to move in frenzied bursts. If the eyelids are gently pulled back, the sleeper appears to be actually witnessing something. The first REM period or dream of the night has begun. Typically, the dream will last for ten minutes. Unfortunately, the dream experience associated with this first REM period is more difficult to recall in the morning. As suddenly as it had begun, the burst of eye activity subsides into the placid rolling of the eyes from side to side—NREM sleep has been re-established.

Thereafter, the process of descent and ascent through the stages of NREM sleep is repeated four to seven times during the night, though we rarely again reach the earlier state of deep sleep. Perhaps that is why sleep in the earlier part of the night is felt to be more refreshing. Each successive REM episode becomes progressively longer, as does the frequency and rapidity of eye movement, so that the final REM phase can last as long as thirty or forty minutes. The average adult has a minimum of four dreams every night, spending about one-and-a-half hours in dreaming sleep. The last dream is generally the one we tend to remember in the morning and is liable to be more elaborate than the earlier dreams of the night.

This research, then, rescues the dream from the hazy realm of speculation surrounding it in the minds of most people. Everyone dreams whether they remember their dreams or not. There are no non-dreamers.

Although there can never be a rigid definition of a dream, empirical investigation has identified certain characteristic features of a dream. Essentially, external sensory information is blocked and the muscles lose their tension so that no dream command can be enacted or any other movement executed, with the exception of eye movements. This, however, does not inhibit the sleeping brain from experiencing motor sensations like walking, running, swimming, even flying. Other cognitive features also continue to function normally. Dreams have a preponderance of visual imagery as also of auditory and tactile sensations, though this sensory information is generated internally. However, taste and smell are not very commonly experienced, nor is pain, even though the dreamer may be involved in dream situations that are frightening. Everything appears real, even though some elements in the dream are bizarre—incongruities (features that do not fit together), discontinuities (changes in time and scene) and identity transformations. But the dreamer does not perceive these elements as bizarre. Instead, he or she is single-mindedly absorbed in the content of the dream and during the dream everything makes sense and is real. There is an absence of self-reflection, and the dreamer has no volitional control over the dream sequence.

Interestingly, a number of American dream researchers

have even suggested that REM sleep warrants recognition as a third basic state of human awareness, thereby confirming the ancient Hindu tradition that consciousness is modified in three distinct ways: *jagrat* (waking), *swapna* (dreaming) and *sushupti* (dreamless sleep).

To recapitulate the difference between them in purely physiological terms: wakefulness is accompanied by fast electrical activity in the brain, by a significant amount of tonus in the muscular system and eye motility. Sleep, or NREM sleep, is characterized by a slackening of electrical activity in the brain, by retention of muscular tension (contrary to our image of the resting body), and the absence of rapid eye movements. Dreaming, or *paradoxical sleep*, presents a more complex picture—brain activity registers as fast waves accompanied by high voltage bursts, and though there is muscular slackness, there are rapid movements in the eyeball muscles.

One may well ask why, if dreams are so closely related to periodically repeated physiological processes, must they have meaning. Do we ascribe meaning to the process of normal digestion? Functionality, yes; but meaning, perhaps not, unless there is an aberration in its functioning. The scientific study of dreams gave rise to a host of theories about the role of dreams. The discovery that there is an inexorable regular periodicity to dreaming led researchers to believe that dreams are a product of physiological processes and nothing else. This fact, coupled with their random and bizarre imagery, made neurologists in the eighties declare that dreaming is essentially meaningless, a wasteland. Our ability to detect a pattern in them is reflective more of our ingenuity than any intentionality of the dream.

Later, based on the emerging computational models of the mind, it became fashionable to explain dreaming in terms of computer functioning.

British psychologist Christopher Evans compared the dreaming brain to a computer that is 'off-line'. The brain absorbs experiences during the day, and while asleep it does not accept any fresh sensory input but sorts and updates its memory files. This process of sorting is what we experience as dreams. It is a necessary and meaningful activity rather like that of the old-fashioned bank clerk who spends the morning depositing and withdrawing money, but then needs the afternoon to update the ledgers.

In 1983, Francis Crick and Graeme Mitchison carried the computational analogy one step further when they proposed their 'reverse learning' theory of dreams. They claimed that due to the brain's limited size, each night it needs to discard information that is occupying space in order to accommodate fresh inputs. Hence their catch phrase, 'We dream in order to forget'. According to them, therefore, dreams are garbage (redundant information) that is excreted by the brain at night—a process of 'reverse learning'. An unimportant snippet from one episode, the tail-end of another, half an opening sequence of a different situation—all compound to form the bizarre dream content. According to this theory, a remembered dream reflects a fundamental error in the dreaming process, and it is then totally nonsensical to attempt to understand the dream.

Opponents of this theory argue that if dreams process past information what, then, dictates the choice of information to be jettisoned? Was there an 'intelligent supervisor' (to use Crick and Mitchison's term) who decrees what to discard and what to retain?

J. Allan Hobson and Robert McCarley, from the Harvard Medical School, proposed an entirely neurophysiological theory of dreaming—the 'activation-synthesis' model. Their goal was to trace the neurological spur of a dream and thereby isolate its biochemical origins. They deduced that dreams are a consequence of 'turning on' a neuronal switch within the brainstem. This 'turning on' bombards the forebrain with neural signals, and *activates* its visual areas thereby generating random images within it. Confronted with these triggered images, the forebrain, which deals with higher functions like thinking, as distinct from the involuntary reflex action of stimulus and response, attempts to *synthesize* them by evoking connected images from its memory banks. This synthesis helps provide the link between the disparate images activated by the neuronal firing in the brainstem, and the synthesized episode is experienced as a dream. This, very briefly, is the Hobson–McCarley model.

Not all researchers, however, subscribe to these hypotheses; they read an entirely different story from the accumulating laboratory data, like evolutionary necessity. Besides physiological or psychological fatigue, there may be other reasons why we sleep. The question then naturally extended to whether animals also exhibit REM in their pattern of sleep.

If every living creature indulges in REM sleep, then a biological function may be attributed to dreaming, like we do to breathing—creatures breathe to live. However, if only some species dream then the purpose of dreaming will have to be sought elsewhere. Research was then extended to elephants, chimpanzees, whales, shrews, pigs, sheep, monkeys, rats, mice, cats, bats, dogs, donkeys, guinea pigs, frogs, alligators, lizards, fish, pigeons, chickens, eagles and snakes among other creatures. It turns out that REM sleep is not exhibited in all creatures. Sleep and dreaming are consistently observed in most if not all mammals, though the patterns vary greatly across them too.

The duration of sleep in mammals ranges from about four to five hours in giraffes and elephants, to eighteen hours or more in bats, opossums and giant armadillos. Smaller mammals need to sleep more than their larger phylogenetic cousins. The length of REM episodes also differs; mammals born immature tend to have more REM sleep, both in infancy and adulthood, than those born mature. Presumably, some of these specific characteristics of sleep and dreaming may have evolved as adaptations to their habitat. For example, marine mammals are sometimes asleep only in one side of their brain, apparently to be able to maintain respiration. If a dolphin is awakened when only one hemisphere is asleep, that hemisphere later shows a sleep rebound (greater need to sleep) while the other one does not. In other words, despite some differences, a recognizable pattern of sleep—cyclically interspersed by dreaming—is evident in all mammals.

In fact, as we go down the evolutionary ladder to the amphibians, even sleep and waking states cannot be clearly demarcated. What is observed is that they merely experience quiescent periods that behaviourally resemble sleep, but it is not clear whether these periods are actual sleep or whether they are simply a form of rest. Reptiles, higher on the evolutionary scale than amphibians, become a point of interest as they are perhaps the earliest species to display mammalian sleep. Some researchers, however, assert that they do not sleep, while others believe they indulge only in NREM sleep, and consequently do not dream. It is thus doubtful whether the reptilian kingdom knows of the circadian rhythm of sleep, a luxury afforded to their more evolved brethren. For the larger mammalian population, their metabolic imperatives, like those of their amphibian predecessors, allow them only a cycle that alternates between activity and rest. Higher up the scale, birds exhibit very well-developed sleep (NREM) and show occasional, very brief (of about a few seconds) episodes of what appears to be an evolutionary precursor of REM sleep. Rarely do they experience reduced muscle tone during the REM phase, and like marine mammals, they also frequently register sleep in only one hemisphere of the brain.

This brief survey shows that dreaming possibly evolved with the advent of mammals from their cold-blooded reptilian ancestors; perhaps the same may be conjectured for sleep also. The point in outlining this research is that it leads to the all-important question: Why did these two events—the advent of mammals and sleep/dreaming—coincide evolutionarily? Do dreams (and sleep) have a biological role in mammalian evolution? Anthony Stevens, in his book *Private Myths: Dreams and Dreaming*, posits that if they are functionally insignificant, 'then they must represent Nature's most stupid blunder and most colossal waste of time'. When an animal is asleep it cannot protect itself from predators, cannot forage for food, cannot procreate, or defend its territory or its young. Yet for over 130 million years, despite enormous evolutionary changes, sleeping and dreaming have persisted in a large number of species. It is likely that sleeping and dreaming are functionally important because despite phylogenetic differences they have ubiquitously persisted in the mammalian world.

An interesting hypothesis advanced by researchers is that mammals, as distinct from amphibians, have eyes on the same side of the head and that rapid eye movement during sleep serves to train mammalian eyes to work together. Amphibian eyes do not have to work together and thus show little or no rapid eye movement during sleep. Intriguing though this thesis is, it surely cannot be the only reason why we dream.

Other researchers posit: Does REM sleep help mature the brain? Coinciding with the apparent introduction of REM sleep in mammals was a remarkable neuro-anatomical change. Initially, brain size had continually increased to accommodate the increased needs of evolutionary advancement. A larger brain could handle more. Strangely we do not find this when we reach the mammals. The brain (prefrontal cortex), rather than enlarge to serve the needs of the more intelligent mammals, reduced in size when compared to the brain of their evolutionary ancestors. Size was perhaps offset by the complexity of functioning. Mammalian brains have more complex networks which service their enhanced needs. An analogous demonstration is the 'brain' of the computer, the chip, which gets smaller continually but is able to 'do' more because of its increased complexity.

But Why Do We Dream?

The conjecture is that REM sleep may have aided the maturational process of the brain. This hypothesis fits in neatly with the research findings in the sleep patterns of the immature young—whether a human baby, a kitten or a puppy. All of them experience a lot more REM sleep when born in comparison to their adult years. For example, the human foetus, when thirty weeks old, spends all its uterine time in REM sleep—complete with eye movements and facial expressions. This complete preoccupation with dreams is sharply reduced to a mere eight hours in a day, or fifty per cent of its sleep, by the time its umbilical connections are cut. This further decreases to three hours of REM sleep by the age of two years and soon afterwards the adult pattern of a little less than two hours (or twenty-five per cent of sleep) is established. It is also a fact that the newborn baby's brain is not fully developed, but reaches full maturity around the same time as REM dreaming starts to decrease. This has led to the hypothesis that REM sleep is connected in some way with the maturation of the brain.

The predominance of REM sleep in early life is not specific to the human baby alone, but is also observed in the newborn puppy, rat and hamster. After birth these young ones, like the human child, take time to reach maturity. One of the exceptions in the mammalian world is the newborn guinea pig who is born mature and whose brain does not develop after birth. The guinea pig exhibits very little REM sleep after birth, thus corroborating our hypothesis. Another confirmation comes from the fact that a premature human baby, whose brain obviously is less developed, spends an increased amount of time (seventy-five per cent) in REM sleep as compared to the normal child. The abundance of REM sleep in infancy raises some difficult questions about the relationship between REM sleep and dreaming. For one, if in the early intrauterine life of the human foetus REM sleep is the all-encompassing mode of existence, then without any life experience to draw from, what could it be dreaming of? Traditional Hindus would, of course, affirm that it is recapitulating its past-life experiences!

Unfortunately, there are no definitive answers as to why we need to sleep and dream; only speculations. Though each of these hypotheses enjoys some experimental support, the mechanism of sleep, and thereby dreaming, is still not wholly understood. Many questions remain unanswered. For all we know there may be no single common function. There are strong indications that sleep is also concerned with homeostasis, that is the maintenance of body or brain temperature, but the exact mechanism is still unclear.

Perhaps sleep and dreams serve an as yet unknown cellular function that supports maturational processes in the young, and/or among other functions, higher mental processes in adult humans. Some researchers believe it plays a role in learning and memory processing. That it is mirrored in physiology does not necessarily preclude meaning. No scientific discovery or research artefact has been able to convincingly demonstrate that dreams do not have any meaning.

How may we then understand the effluvia of the night? Humanists insist that any phenomenon experienced by people warrants attention and that, sometimes, a dream can provide insights so novel and rewarding that it feels ungracious not to regard the dream as an intentional communication of some sort.

There is thus an unyielding mystery at the heart of a dream. It is in trying to unravel this mystery that many schools of thought have arisen. Each theory propounded—from antiquity to modern times—is an attempt to grapple with a few simple questions about dreams: Where do they come from? Why are they so strange (bizarre)? What function(s) do they serve? And, of course, what do they mean?

The earliest conception of dreams in antiquity held that the source of dreams were the gods or the supernatural world. Dreams were strange because gods spoke in parables. Their function was to guide, warn and inspire man to realize his destiny. An uninterpreted dream was like an unopened letter, its message ignored.

In direct contrast are modern scientific theories, which rely on brain chemistry to answer these very questions. They trace the source of dreams to the neural activity in the brain stem. Their strangeness is attributed to a medley of imperfectly assimilated images, randomly generated as a by-product of periodic neuronal firing within the sleeping brain. Their function is the daily clean-up of the brain's neural circuitry. They are not meant to be interpreted, as there is no inherent meaning in them. Whatever we 'read' into them is only a secondary effect of waking thought, superimposed upon an episode recalled after awakening.

Away from explanations that place in the centre gods or brain neurology stands Freud, who treated dreams neither as simply an activity of the brain nor as having an external source, but as an internal psychic event that arose from the unconscious. The unconscious—being the submerged and internal part of the human psyche that controls all conscious behaviour—was equated neither with an external god nor with the brain. For Freud, and many subsequent theorists, it remains the source of all dreams. And dreams are strange because they are a disguise wrought by the psyche to mask an unacceptable and therefore repressed wish, which is usually sexual. Their function was to preserve sleep, and the method used to interpret them was to reverse their disguise with the help of a chain of free associations. Free associations can be made when any train of thought is allowed to come to mind without its flow being impeded by logic or reasoning. This can uncover that ungratified, infantile longing of which the dream was but a distorted expression.

In all these theories, attention has been paid to the dream's lack of conformance with mundane reality—the strangeness of the dream, or what is called dream-bizarreness. The ancient world attributed dream-bizarreness to the imperfect understanding of man, who was unable to comprehend God's language, and hence dreams had to convey his message through riddles. The scientific world, confronted with the illogicality of dreams, declared that they were essentially meaningless. And it was this bizarreness of the dream that Freud's perception—that the dream is a disguise of a repressed desire—was founded on.

The way we answer those fundamental questions theorists have reflected on for centuries is bound to affect our method of interpreting a dream. Maybe this can be illustrated with Calpurnia's oft-repeated dream in *Julius*

Caesar: She saw 'Caesar's statue which like a fountain with an hundred spouts did run blood'. She was convinced she had dreamt of Caesar's assassination: 'Thrice hath Calpurnia in her sleep cried out, "Help, ho! They murder Caesar!"' More than the *truth* of her dream images, it was her historical context that made her believe that the dream was an obvious prognostication intended to safeguard the life of her husband. She was being *told* to restrain Caesar from attending the Senate.

With dreams considered to be messages from an external source, the ancient world restricted their function to pronouncements about an unforeseeable future. Hence it was important to dream about victory before the war, of game before the hunt. In fact, Decius duplicitously tells Caesar that Calpurnia's dream indicates victories for Rome promising that 'from you great Rome shall suck reviving blood...'

Both interpretations view the dream as a prognostication despite the fact that they draw different meanings from the same dream.

On the other hand, had Calpurnia lived in modern times, her analyst would have led her through a psychological labyrinth of infantile urges to comprehend her dream: she was expecting to find a replica of her father in her spouse, and finding him lacking actually wished his death; or they would treat it as a therapeutic device that promised psychological health to Calpurnia's marriage.

We somehow expect that a dream should have only one 'true' interpretation. Which meaning would be the *right* one of Calpurnia's dream? How can a network of meanings reside in dreams? History has not only substantiated Calpurnia's interpretation, but it has also justified Decius's rendering of the dream. The Roman legions under Augustus—Julius Caesar's successor—did subsequently fan out and revive Roman hegemony over the Mediterranean and much of Europe, ushering in the Golden Age of Rome. Further, we cannot really limit the dream to being a mere personal and social prophecy, foretelling the fate of Caesar and Rome. It would not be too far-fetched to see the psychological truth of the dream as well. After all, Caesar had not exactly walked the straight and narrow path of matrimony; he had reputedly sired a son by Cleopatra. Besides, his ambition laced with his megalomania must have translated into pretty selfish behaviour at home, robbing Calpurnia of any form of companionship. Her dream may very well have been an expression of her deep marital dissatisfaction and their bleeding, dying relationship. Of course, we can never know whether Calpurnia actually did dream of Caesar's death, or whether it was simply a literary device employed by the creative genius of Shakespeare, or Plutarch for that matter!

~

The Jewish scholar Rabbi Binza reported that he once consulted twenty-four dream interpreters who were in Jerusalem at one time and received different interpretations of his dream from each, all of which were subsequently realized.

Specialists have tended to submerge the dream within a superstructure, such that only a trained professional could locate its meaning. Others have questioned this belief arguing that the dream really belongs to the dreamer and

But Why Do We Dream?

to no one else. Therefore he or she is the best person to decode it; thereby freeing the dream from the clinic and giving ownership back to the dreamer. Can't any person, with a little familiarization, learn to interpret his or her own dreams?

3. What's This Dream Telling Me?

I intend to sketch out a simple method to provide a framework for understanding a dream. It is not a definitive method, or a standard formula for handling every type of dream. Special knowledge about dreams is not required, nor is any training necessary; all that is needed is a fascination with dreams, peppered with a healthy dose of curiosity. And once readers become familiar with the language of dreams, they should adopt a technique that suits them best. This is but a scaffolding, which needs to be dismantled once the reader gets the 'feel' of interpreting dreams.

Most of us, when confronted with our dreams, fail to make sense of them because they speak in a language which largely comprises of visual imagery. This form of communication usually does not directly portray the dreamer's real-life situation. Could our puzzlement be because the dream is a metaphorical communication about our concerns?

This metaphorical communication can be interpreted in multiple ways which adds to the inherent difficulty of making sense of our dreams. Take for example the colour blue. In a dream it can allude to pornography, aristocracy, grief, freedom, or infinity, underscoring the many unrelated directions that the interpretation may take. It leaves the dreamer wondering whether there is any one accurate interpretation.

We routinely use metaphors and symbols in our speech and thought—boiling mad, or trophy wife, or winter of life. Often the boundaries between a symbol and a metaphor overlap. To simplify dream interpretation, I am intentionally separating symbols from metaphors which are essentially two different aspects of the dream. Most dreams have a storyline—a plot—which unfolds as the dream progresses. As in a play or novel, a host of characters enact the plot, but the thematic content is distinct from it. Similarly, a dream may have many symbols (the characters), but together these symbols allude to a particular theme—its *metaphorical* message. So, a dream speaks in the language of symbols but conveys its meaning through metaphors. Working within the dreamer's specific life context, these metaphors unfold the complex feelings buried in the dream. A metaphorical mode of dream communication perhaps best reflects the range of emotions we experience. A woman's dream of a stillborn child, for example, expresses her feelings of disappointment and failed expectations far more powerfully than words can. A person who dreams that his car is hurtling down a cliff will experience the sensation of being in an uncontrollably dangerous situation far more potently than ordinary language can convey.

Comprehending metaphors depends on one's ability to see an implicit similarity between things that are otherwise dissimilar. The metaphorical element makes the dream appear strange or bizarre, but it certainly grabs our attention. Every dream will have one or more such elements that beckon for attention—perhaps an obvious incongruity, a powerful emotion or a motif.

That is easily said, but a welter of confusion confronts us when we come across contradictory images in a dream. To exemplify this, a person dreamt of a cactus growing on the North Pole—the sheer oddity of it! However, there is a powerful metaphor in this bizarre dream—a cactus is found in hot deserts, while the North Pole is a cold desert. By amplifying the image of a desert, is the dreamer being alerted to its many meanings—being jilted, feeling alone or abandoned?

Of course, the personal associations of the dreamer to the dream images are of paramount importance to highlight the specific area of the dreamer's life being referred to. We cannot hope to rely on a dictionary of set meanings since metaphors are created based on the dreamer's ability to form connections between two seemingly disconnected things. If no associations are triggered, the best way to approach a dream is to focus on the feelings evoked by the dream imagery and connect them to waking concerns. This process has been likened to forming a *bridge* from the images in the dream to something in the dreamer's life.

Suppose in a dream you find yourself on a battlefield, oblivious to the shells and bullets flying around you. Unless you are a soldier on furlough this may not represent your real-life situation. In order to understand the message of the dream you may have to form a bridge from the dream to your actual situation. This can be done by asking yourself which feelings predominated your experience of the dream, or which were conspicuously absent. In the example above the dreamer is unaffected amidst a dangerous situation—an inappropriate feeling within the context of the dream. You may then need to find a connection between the dream emotion and a life situation. A moment in the past or present that others regarded as dangerous but you did not. Or perhaps the question could be: What dangerous situation are you in that you were unaware of?

The identification of the metaphor immediately makes the message of the dream transparent. Dreams can have a single- or a multi-metaphor theme. In a multi-metaphor dream, it is advisable to determine the main or lead metaphor. The others then become secondary to it. Once the lead metaphor is established the rest of the images are interpreted around it. Even if sequential scenes are disparate, we will still have to identify the metaphorical thread that sews the scenes into a single theme.

Perhaps a few examples, starting with a very simple single-metaphor dream may elucidate the process. 'Mala Saxena'[1] dreamt:

> *I get into my car, but much to my horror realize that the car has no steering wheel.*

The dream vividly conveys that Mala is unable to direct her car, or some aspect of her life. The main metaphor in the dream is the steering wheel; its absence has, possibly, caused her lack of direction. It was Mala who provided the bridge to her feeling adrift. 'I lost my father six months ago. He was not just a father to me. He was a friend, an advisor, in fact, my mentor.'

Another example. 'Sanjay Dhir' dreamt:

I'm on a cricket field where I am expected to bowl. I make my way towards the bowling run-up but suddenly realize that the pitch looks much longer than the usual twenty-two yards. I begin to feel unsure about my ability to bowl effectively on such a long pitch. But when I approach the bowling crease I find that the pitch is a normal one, and suddenly feel capable of giving a good delivery.

The dominant metaphor in this dream is the pitch, and the dreamer's reaction to it is expressed through two emotions, that appear sequentially. Initially, there is a feeling of inadequacy that later changes to confidence. This is the dream of a father whose young child needed surgery, which was possible only in a town that was unfamiliar to him. He was worried about who he would turn to if the need arose. In fact, he was uncertain on many counts. The dream describes his anxiety through a cricket pitch—*it is too long for an effective delivery*. However, there is reassurance in the dream that once he gets into the situation—when he nears the crease—he sees that it's not so bad, and he will be able to cope.

Sanjay had this dream before he left for the surgery and I heard him relate the dream, post the operation, in a workshop on dreams. The operation had been successful, his son improved steadily and before long they were back home.

In trying to understand these dreams, we first identified their metaphorical statements, located their central theme and then related them to something in the dreamer's life. But what happens in a long, meandering dream? Would it be easy to identify its central metaphor? The following is the dream of a young boy, 'Manish Chawla', who is soon to enter his teens:

> We are playing marbles during the lunch recess when a lion roars into the school compound. We all run into the school building and hide. He frightens us—he is on a rampage, destroying everything. My friend is confused: He cannot even see us, nor did we tease him, so why is he so angry? Suddenly my father arrives in the school with his twelve-bore gun. Though I am very relieved I don't go up to him, because I am afraid to let him see that I'm actually scared.
>
> My father goes out into the courtyard, and I quietly follow him, without his knowledge. He fires twice at the lion, but to my surprise nothing happens to it. Dad quickly reloads the gun and shoots. I can see the bullet as it speeds towards the lion's head. The lion just stands on his hind legs and eats the bullet. All that happens is that his mane of hair slips back so that instead of being at his neck it is now around the lower part of his stomach, and his two hind legs have become wheels. This enables him to come towards us faster. Before my father can reload his gun, the lion swallows us both.
>
> I open my eyes to find my father massaging my neck where the lion had bit it. He is not annoyed with me for following him, but says that I must not make any noise as we are in the stomach of the lion and he must not know that we are alive. We start moving very quietly through the valleys and mountains, keeping an eye out for wild animals. After a long,

long time we are able to cut our way out of the lion's stomach with the help of a hunting knife.

The scene changes, my father and I are watching a Bharatanatyam dance performance. I think the other people must think that our clothes, after the adventure we have been through, are smelly and full of blood. But they don't seem to notice. I look at my clothes and am stunned to find that we are actually nicely dressed for the occasion. Even I am wearing a dark suit and necktie and my shoes are perfectly polished. Had I imagined the lion, or were we watching a dance that had a lion? No, I am sure, we were not imagining the lion. I turn again to look at the stage—all the performers are girls.

Then he woke up.

At first glance this seems a rambling, meaningless dream of an adolescent boy without any structure or storyline. However, to make sense of it we can divide the dream into its component scenes: an angry lion enters the school compound; the father attempts to subdue it; instead, the lion swallows the father–son duo but they manage to escape from the lion's stomach; and finally, the boy finds himself attending a dance recital. With this break-up it is easier to identify that there are two metaphors running through the dream. The first is a boy's encounter with a lion, and the second is the father's role in this drama. Which of the two is the primary metaphor? The lion dominates the dream, and the thematic content of the plot hinges on it, while the father's role is dependent on the lion and may, therefore, be considered the secondary metaphor.

Making a bridge from the lead metaphor—the lion—to something in Manish's life, may elucidate the meaning of the dream. It was difficult to get any kind of association from him. However, I was struck by the way he pronounced 'lion': *'a loin roars into the school...speeds towards the loin's head...the loin just stands on his hind legs...'* Unwittingly, he had provided the clue: the lion was actually the *loins*. Trying to use this lead to make the bridge we may ask: Is the main metaphor about sexual awakening? Was the dream pointing to Manish's first encounter with his libido? Had the full force of its awakening burst upon him, like the dramatic entry of the lion in the dream? Sexual awakening at puberty is often felt as an alien, powerful force, erupting into a boy's consciousness as something fearful, awe-inspiring and uncontrollable—similar to Manish's reaction to the lion in the dream.

Once it has been established that the dream is about puberty, it is easier to comprehend why the lion is on a rampage, uncontrolled within the school compound, indicative of instinctive urges running riot within the enclosure of Manish's personal world—his thoughts.

The dream opens with Manish and his friends playing marbles, a boyish inclination before the advent of puberty. His friend's perplexity about the unreasonableness of the lion, perhaps, points to the bewilderment Manish faced with the build-up in his instinctual life.

Manish is relieved at the father's arrival, but is hesitant to greet him in case his quailing legs betray his internal confusion. But this hesitation does not detract him from wilfully trailing behind his father towards the lion. This aptly captures a pubescent boy's ambivalent attitude towards his parents and especially the father. Boys are not apt to talk about this emerging experience of puberty with their fathers; yet he is the only one, the dream tells us, who wields a gun. The dream further tells us that the father's bullets (parental guidance) bounce off; the lion (the pubescent boy) is impervious to them. If we had any residual doubt about the symbolic significance of the dream, then the depiction of the lion that follows should dispel it—the mane slips back to present a hairless member raising itself: an erect 'loin'.

In the next scene, the lion swallowing Manish symbolically states that to attain maturity the boy has to 'die' to his childhood ways. In the process, the father would also be swallowed by the lion, implying that his current relationship with his father has to change. The father–son duo journeying together in the lion's stomach indicates that it will take some time for this change to be assimilated by Manish; the 'battle' lies ahead of him. It is not only reflective of biological changes and psychological re-evaluations, but every aspect of his life would undergo transformation. They would be able to cut their way out of the lion's belly only when he is ready to be 'reborn'.

It seems that Manish's dream of being swallowed and the subsequent transformation was neither all that bizarre nor personal to him. This is a universally recurrent image found in the myths and legends of many cultures. The hero, instead of conquering or being able to placate the powers that oppose him, is swallowed by them. Hiawatha, the American Indian chief, and his canoe were swallowed by Mishe-Nahma—the King of Fishes. The Inuit of the Bering

Strait tell the tale of their hero Raven being swallowed by a whale, and how he then stood inside its belly and looked around; the Zulus have a story of a mother and her two children, in which an elephant swallows the mother. In the European fairy tale of Red Riding Hood, she was swallowed by a wolf.

Returning to the specifics in the dream we find that the main metaphor of the lion—the instinctual turbulence of puberty—is intertwined with the secondary metaphor: the father. The dream-father is a symbol of the guiding voice that the young boy so desperately needs now. Suddenly, Manish's relationship with the father changes after the lion has swallowed them. The latter is massaging his neck instead of scolding him for following him. Now they are journeying together. The boy becomes a junior apprentice to the father. Later in the dream we witness still another change in their relationship when they emerge from this ordeal and sit together, like two adults, at the dance performance. The archetypal father's influence extends far beyond the process of Manish's sexual maturation; he acts as the bridge between the individual and the collective, between family and society. All that Manish notices, after emerging from the encounter with the 'loin', is that the dance performance is filled with girls—perhaps an apt testimony to what pervades his pubescent mind. However, he is expected to sublimate his emerging sexuality, as evidenced in the dream by his distant participation as a member of the audience.

Manish has metamorphosed from someone playing the boyish games of marbles into an adult engaged in a considerably more sophisticated pursuit. He is now transformed into a new life.

I am not for a moment suggesting that Manish, or any other pubescent boy, is able to articulate all this to himself; his consciousness is crammed with great question marks looming in every direction. He simply tries to cope with what is arising out of his being. He will get hurt, stumble and learn and rise again, all the while groping to understand what he is supposed to do, and whether he will be able to do it well.

The unravelling of young Manish's dream was simplified because we were able to identify its lead metaphor and the secondary ones. It seems that the skill, or the art, in grasping a dream lies in deciding which metaphor is most important. No hard and fast rules govern this, but generally a few important features could help draw attention to the main metaphor in your dream. The golden rule is not to hunt for the metaphors; let them attract your attention. Let them speak to you. There will always be some element, or elements, in the dream demanding to be heard, and they may do so in a variety of ways.

Possibly, the easiest to spot is an obvious incongruity, as in Mala's dream, where the steering wheel of the car was missing. Take another dream example: a woman is walking her dog in the park. Nothing in the dream stands out. However, if the woman is, say, Indira Gandhi or Jackie Kennedy, then this metaphor attracts attention, and the dream interpretation will be built around it. Alternatively, if the dog bites a passer-by, then this particular aspect would assume significance and the interpretation would lead in a different direction. The trouble begins if the woman is Mrs Gandhi and the dog also bites a passer-by. Then we would have to accord relative importance to the competing metaphors, like we did to the lion and the father in Manish's dream, and knit the two metaphors together to arrive at an interpretation.

Another way in which a dream element assumes prominence is by repetition. If the dog continues to bite every passer-by, then it certainly will deserve special attention. Or say the woman stops every now and then to ask the passers-by, 'Do you get messages from the Unconscious?' Then the bizarre nature of the question, and not the woman, will merit attention. However, if the sentence is a standard pleasantry—'Have a good day'—then it is not important and cannot be considered the lead metaphor.

Another form of repetition that attracts attention is the recurrence of a symbol. The woman may not be Mrs Gandhi and the dog may not bite, but if night after night you dreamt that a woman is walking her dog in the park—the same woman, the same dog in the neighbourhood park—the sequence, by its sheer recurrence, will cry out for attention. The dream may even assume a reality that compels you to contemplate verifying whether such a woman or a similar dog do actually frequent the nearby park. Similarly, a metaphor recurring in dream after dream alerts you to its significance.

What happens when there is no incongruity, repetition or recurrence? Continuing with our example of the lady walking in the park, if none of the attention-grabbing devices are present in the dream, and the woman is the dreamer's neighbour and her dog is a placid creature, we could attempt to identify the metaphorical allusion by asking the dreamer if there's any overriding trait in the neighbour that comes to mind. We could ask the dreamer to try and characterize the neighbour. This may then lead us towards the significance of the dream. If, for instance, the response is that the neighbour is very organized, then the dream is asking the dreamer to look at the decisive/scattered aspects in his or her own life, perhaps as regards routine activities (the dog has to be walked every day). It is obvious that it is the perception of the neighbour and not their actual traits that is critical to the association.

If the neighbour is just a name in the phone book, with no personal involvement, then her name may provide the clue. If it is Asha, it could allude to hope, if Nirmala, to cleanliness. We do not have to restrict ourselves to the people in the dream. If the neighbour has not registered in the dreamer's memory in any way and her name does not ring any bells, we could explore the associations with the dog, or with dogs in general, and make a bridge from those attributes to something in the dreamer's life. As always, the association of the dreamer is most important and holds the key to the dream.

~

Numbers appearing in a dream need not be representative only of age; there are many ways of understanding their significance as the following dream shows. Immediately after getting his Senior Cambridge exam results, my husband Rajeev dreamt:

> *A school friend is with me and we go to the market to buy cloth for a shirt. The cloth costs three rupees, but the stitching charges for the shirt are twenty-one rupees! We find this very puzzling.*

He related it to an uncle who was interested in dreams, adding that dreams do get things mixed up; it might have been more realistic had the cloth in the dream cost twenty-one rupees and the stitching charges were only three rupees.

The uncle replied, 'If that were so, then the dream would be telling you nothing.'

'But what is it saying?'

His uncle was silent for a while then said, 'You are puzzled about your school results. There is something you don't agree with, or are surprised about.'

Rajeev was taken aback as the school had just communicated the results by post and he hadn't told his uncle anything.

His uncle continued, 'It seems you are puzzled about scoring a three in some subject.'

Rajeev said he felt he had done better in the physics exam than in chemistry and was surprised at getting a grade 2 in chemistry and a 3 in physics. He was happy about the chemistry result, but he felt that he deserved at least a grade 2 in physics.

A few days later, a letter came from the school apologizing for an error in communicating Rajeev's results. The grades were corrected to a 2 in physics and a 3 in chemistry. Needless to say, Rajeev confronted the uncle with the letter, asking, 'How did you do it? Magic?'

'Your dream was screaming it loud and clear, but you thought it was about prices in the real world. By presenting an anomaly it was drawing your attention to the number 3. The cloth was for three rupees and the stitching charge of twenty-one can also be read as two plus one, which is again a three.'

There is something impressive when a dream is interpreted in this fashion, and it seems Rajeev's uncle had the knack for it. He was quick to spot the number as the lead metaphor, and the repetition of the number 3 in the dream helped him identify the cause for concern in Rajeev's teenage mind. However, most dreams are difficult to interpret in this manner: Rajeev's uncle had provided the bridge intuitively, without asking him for his associations. This is possible only if the interpreter knows the dreamer well, and is well versed with his or her concerns.

~

Needless to say that before we embark on the adventure of interpreting our dreams, it is important to remember them. The best way to start remembering your dreams is to tell yourself every night before you drift into sleep: I will remember my dream tonight.

I recall my Teacher introducing someone to dreams.

Promptly came the reply, 'But I don't dream.'

My Teacher ignored the objection and continued to discuss late into the night the significance of dreams and how to record them.

Next morning, the man in question reported with astonishment, 'I had six dreams last night! And I was able to write them down.'

A little interest in the subject had stimulated the dreaming mind to respond. If you are interested in your dreams, maintain a notebook and pen by your bedside specifically to record them. Before going to sleep, write down the date on a fresh page. If ever you awaken during the night, write down whatever comes to you—even if it is only a mood, or an image. If you do not write down the dream immediately, any memory of it would probably disappear by the morning.

Upon waking, train yourself not to open your eyes immediately, but to dwell on any dream feelings or images that you can recall. In order to focus, lie quietly, do not move or change position, or switch on the light. However small the fragment that you remember, undistracted, just stay with the dream. Try and relive the mood of the dream images.

If, even after a few days of trying, you are unable to recollect your dreams, then don't bother recalling them. Instead, aim to recollect what you had been thinking of at the moment of waking and then try to find out why you were thinking those thoughts. This process may lead you to the memory of a dream, after which, like an angler, you can reel in the other segments of the dream.

It is important to record a dream as close to the time it happened, otherwise one might lose the details, or forget large chunks of it. After writing down the dream, record your feelings. What was the most dominant emotion? Write down any associations you may have with the dream images—people, situations or objects in the dream. With these associations in mind ask yourself: What is the symbolic story that the dream is telling me and what could it be referring to within my current life situation?

If you're having trouble interpreting your dreams, don't worry. Keep the dream diary going. Rest assured that the most important dream dictionary is the one you will produce by keeping a dream journal. After a month, re-read the dreams. You may find that most of them are centred on one particular theme. The common thread through them may help you clarify a dream you were unable to understand earlier. As my teacher Ashishda used to say, the dreaming intelligence presents the same theme from many perspectives in an attempt to help us see the situation from various angles. It tells us: 'Look at it this way.' If we can't, then it says, 'Hey, what about this angle? Got it?' Once we're able to grasp the issue then it may build on our understanding by giving us many more insights and further information. This dreaming intelligence is also very gentle with us, especially when we are struggling with something that is difficult to cope with. It may say, 'I suppose that's enough for the time being. We'll come back to this subject a little later. Let's talk of something else.' And it will start on a new series of dreams.

Many of our dreams portray and comment on our everyday concerns, which is why it is necessary to try to arrive at the relevant waking experiences that could have triggered a dream. Try to remember what you were thinking of before going to sleep, because that can often be an important clue. If this does not give you the lead to the dream imagery, then think back in detail to all you did on the day preceding the dream. Forming the bridge between dream imagery and our waking life is key to helping us fathom the intricate messages our dreams are trying to convey.

4. Why Do We Keep Dreaming the Same Dreams?

I have been noting my dreams for four decades and frequent among them are anxiety dreams, which relay my concerns and my perceived inability to cope with a situation at hand. Listening to the dreams of others made me realize that such themes were also present in their dreams.

In the 1950s and 1960s, Calvin Hall, an American psychologist and dream researcher, collected and categorized dreams and their contents from a large number of subjects from around the world. He, along with Vernon Nordby, examined over 50,000 dreams and concluded that a number of 'typical' themes are represented over and over again.[1] Hall and Nordby believed that virtually every dreamer experiences these typical dreams. It may be said that they constitute the universal constants of the human psyche, expressing the shared concerns, preoccupations and interests of all dreamers. Hall's studies indicate that dreams of being pursued are one of the two most common kinds of dreams, the other being the 'falling' dream.

This would imply that these dreams are not personal to the dreamer but reflect common concerns. I am not arguing in favour of dream dictionaries of yore, which usually allocated a standard meaning to symbols and unlocked every element in the dream by one 'key'. This position has been long reversed by Freud's revolutionary suggestion that 'The only dictionary we need to decode our dreams is not on our bookshelves but in our heads'. The meaning of a dream could be located by the free associations of the dreamer to the different elements in the dream.

However, Freud also noted that there were certain dreams that almost everyone dreamt alike. He concluded that these emanated from the same source and presumably had the same meaning. Such dreams, as a rule, failed to produce any associations which would ordinarily help in decoding them. This led to the identification of the *typical* dream, and most analysts agree on the validity of using a common approach to their meaning.

These typical themes include sitting for an examination, missing a train, being pursued by a hostile stranger or predatory animal, falling from a great height, flying, finding oneself naked in company or having one's teeth fall out.

The dream themes discussed below are not an exhaustive exploration of typical dreams. Some of the themes mentioned—like flying and sex—may not fall strictly under the category of anxiety dreams, but their constant occurrence and the interest that so many people have in them warrants their inclusion.

Being Chased

I'm being chased by a band of robbers. I'm running fast in a dark alley, with my pursuers gaining ground. Their footsteps are as loud as galloping horses. My heart is pounding more with fear than exertion as I

*try and zigzag my way without looking back. I just
keep running from the threat, which may overwhelm
me any moment...*

Dreams of being chased are accompanied by a great sense of dread. The pursuer is mostly a threatening person, a wild animal, or in some cases even a ghost. Normally, the dreamer does not offer any kind of resistance, either by turning around to face the pursuer or by fighting back. And interestingly, the pursuer never actually overwhelms the dreamer, but the threat is unremitting. The dreamer's terror usually ends by awakening from the dream.

Hall's survey in the mid-fifties of 517 American college students found that ninety-three per cent of the males and ninety-eight per cent of the females had had one or both of these dreams of being chased or falling from a height. In analysing the content of 106 such dreams he found that in dreams of being chased, both men and women typically dreamed of an unprovoked physical attack by a male to which the dreamer responded by fleeing.[2]

Hall believed that when such dreams appear, typified by a display of poor resistance, they represent the dreamer's self-conception of being a weak, passive, inferior or helpless person. This low self-image could be attributed to threatening external circumstances. According to other psychologists, the pursuer is not necessarily an external threat, but is representative of the fact that the dreamer's feelings are slipping out of control. As such, these dreams could also be projections of 'disowned parts of the dreamer's personality'.

Dreams provide one of the most effective ways to confront an anxiety or fear. Most of our anxieties can be attributed to something that we find difficult to face. Rather than accept them as situations that demand resolution, we project them as external threats, like a stranger stalking us in a dream. Oftentimes, anxiety is not amenable to reason, and the accumulation of free-floating anxieties slowly turns into an unidentifiable fear. An anxious thought may subside temporarily when the associated threat recedes. When more entrenched, the anxiety can resurface with greater vehemence than before. Such dreams prompt us to examine our feelings and states of mind.

Do anxiety dreams serve a purpose? To answer this question, researchers from the University of Geneva (UNIGE) and Geneva University Hospitals (HUG), Switzerland, working in collaboration with the University of Wisconsin, USA, analysed the dreams of a number of people and identified which areas of the brain were activated when they experienced fear in their dreams. They found that once the individual woke up, the brain areas responsible for controlling emotions responded to fear-inducing situations more effectively. These results, which are published in the journal *Human Brain Mapping*, demonstrated that dreams help us react better to frightening situations, thereby paving the way for combating anxiety more effectively in waking life. This also reinforces a neuroscientific theory about dreams: we simulate frightening situations while dreaming in order to better react to them once we are awake.[3]

Here I would like to cite the example of the Senoi people—a tribal community in the mountainous jungles of Malaysia—who are said to teach their children the art of dreaming. In recent times, the theory of dreams ascribed to them has come under strong criticism because the anthropological research backing it has been dubbed suspect—even fabricated. But it is worth mentioning due to its psychological relevance.

The Senoi, it is claimed, teach their children that nocturnal adversaries, typically encountered in dreams, are hostile spirits that, when confronted and overcome, transform into healing ones. If a child were to recall being chased by a tiger and fleeing in terror in a dream, the father would invariably urge them not to run the next time they dreamt of being chased. They should learn to stand their ground, and moreover, slowly turn around to confront the tiger. With these repeated injunctions, gradually, the child might be able to do so in the dream and look the beast in the face and ask: What do you want?

One may or may not believe in hostile or helping spirits, but a very important psychological truth seems embedded in these simple practices. They force the dreamer to confront a fear at its root—the unconscious. Our anxieties and fears, if left unchecked, can devour us. If you face the tiger in the dream, you may find that you are able to confront the underlying threat in waking life, be it a difficult boss, a messy relationship, or a debtor at the doorstep.

If our dream figures represent internalized ideas about ourselves and others, then the effort we make in changing our reaction to them in our dreams may alter the way we interact with our waking environment, thereby transforming our ideas about our self and the world.

Falling

Dreamers often experience a steep fall through space—from a cliff, from the top of a high-rise building or from a window—this being attended by an acute sense of panic or fear. An abrupt awakening on the part of the dreamer, before hitting the ground, usually terminates such a dream.

Schools of thought differ on what these dreams could symbolize. The physiological school explains them simply as the transition from wakefulness into sleep. As we fall asleep, the brain produces a steady alpha rhythm[4] in which the pulse and breath rate slow down, the body temperature drops, and the sleeper enters fully into Stage 1 of sleep, a state of deep relaxation. This school believes that no metaphorical meaning should be attached to these dreams since they represent the bodily sensation of releasing control during the onset of sleep. 'Falling asleep' or 'dropping off to sleep' are common expressions that describe this process somewhat literally. Research indicates that women report falling dreams more frequently than men during this stage of onset of sleep.

Frederic Myers, a pioneering British explorer of the unconscious, termed the dreams that precede sleep *hypnogogic* and dreams that come just as we are awakening *hypnopompic*. Falling, tripping or stepping off a kerb accidentally are all images associated with hypnogogic dreams that come as we drift from waking into sleep.

Freud disagreed with the somatic explanation. He felt that falling dreams are the reproduction of childhood games involving movement, which are very attractive to children. He believed that there cannot be a single child who has not been held aloft and made to 'fly' across the room, or who has not been thrown up in the air and experienced the sudden drop before it is caught again. Children are delighted by such experiences and never tire of having them repeated. Freud says, 'In after years they repeat these experiences in dreams; but in the dreams they leave out the hands which held them up, so that they float or fall unsupported.'

In complete contrast to the physiological theory and Freud's kinetic-sexual basis of falling dreams is the theory where falling is treated as a symbol and interpreted as such. Downward motion often has negative connotations: we *fall* short on a job; we *fall* into the enemy's hands; we *fall* upon hard times; we *fall* into bad ways or *fall* from grace. In a falling dream we have 'lost our balance'. Falling dreams are thus generally considered to represent situations in which the dreamer experiences loss of control, is helpless, in danger of losing his or her status in someone's eyes, or fears the loss of security or emotional stability.

Flying

In this kind of dream, the dreamer is flying unaided through the air. In contrast to falling dreams, flying dreams bring a remarkable sense of exhilaration. Rarely are flying dreams experienced as unpleasant or fearful, for they bring with them a sense of freedom and exultation wherein dreamers feel empowered and in complete control of their actions. Speaking of the experience of flying, some dreamers relate it as if it were a strange recognition of a skill that they had always possessed, but forgotten how to use.

These are not restricted to solo flights—there can be

other people—strangers, friends or guides—accompanying the dreamer. You may find that you are running hard in a dream and then suddenly, without any warning, you are airborne and flying. Or you may be in the air from the start of the dream, flying like a bird, or cutting through the air with arms straight out like a superhero, or just floating high above the rooftops, sailing in the air as you observe the world below.

Flying has connotations of 'flying high', of being successful, of feeling elated, also of being ambitious and achievement-oriented. Many people have reported that the 'high' from a flying dream can last for several days. Literally, the sky is the limit, and sometimes they find themselves going even beyond, into space and among the stars. Anjali Hazarika, a corporate consultant who uses dream work in her training programmes for managers, says in her book, *Daring to Dream*, 'I flew for days in my dreams after I got a first class in my postgraduate degree course in Psychology.'

Examinations

> *I am sitting for an examination and the invigilator hands me the question paper. I read through all the questions. To my complete horror I do not know the answer to any of them.*

'Arvind Mehra' had this dream on the eve of a presentation he had to make for an advertising campaign that he had been working on for days.

It is amazing how many people have complained of the obstinacy with which they have been pursued by the dream of failure in an examination. There are many variations: the dreamer arrived late for the examination, the wretched pen would not work, the dreamer had studied for the wrong exam, or could not finish the exam in the allotted time. The irony is that many of these dreamers have successfully negotiated school and college examinations and are now themselves doctors, university professors or top executives.

The term 'examination dream' is also used to describe situations in which the dreamer has to deliver a talk and suddenly becomes speechless; is cast in a play and cannot remember the lines; or says something utterly inappropriate to what is being asked. The commonality in all these dreams is that the person feels inadequate, ill-prepared and fears failure or the disapproval of others.

Examination dreams may coincide with transitional phases in our life, for example, when we are judging our professional competence, when we feel unready to meet personal challenges like moving house, becoming a parent or even qualifying for a driving license. A man who was preparing for his daughter's forthcoming marriage related an examination dream, which given the circumstances in India is indeed a trying experience!

These are not veridical dreams, warning or predicting a particular outcome. Arvind Mehra's inability to perform in the dream was not a comment on his presentation. All it testified to was his anxiety about an impending situation. In fact, Wilhelm Stekel, a gifted Austrian physician and psychologist, who was one of Freud's earliest followers, but who later moved away from him and developed his own 'active analytic therapy', said that 'dreams of Matriculation only occur in people who have successfully passed it and never in people who have failed in it'. It seems that the anxiety-filled examination dreams appear when the dreaming mind, in order to reassure the dreamer, searches for some experience in the past in which the anxiety turned out to be unjustified. Freud himself mentions how he had failed in Forensic Medicine in his finals, but had never dreamt of that particular exam. He says in *The Interpretation of Dreams*, 'In my dreams of school examinations I am invariably examined in History, in which I did brilliantly…'

Missing a Train

Similar to the examination dream is the dream in which a person misses a train. These dreams are frequently reported and thus warrant separate mention. 'Malini Chandra' dreamt:

> *I am running down the steps that lead to the railway platform. Halfway down the staircase I see the train pulling out of the platform. I charge down two stairs at a time, trying desperately to weave my way through the throng of people. By the time I reach the platform I can see the last coach ahead of me. I run as fast as I can. The train gathers speed, leaving me standing breathless and anxious on the platform.*

A familiar dream for many of us. It could be a missed bus, boat or aeroplane—but the theme remains the same. It could even extend to missing an appointment, or misplacing your luggage.

These dreams of arriving too late may be seen as

'frustration dreams'. Generally, these dreams alert the dreamer that some resource is being depleted and the effort to properly adapt to external circumstances is being forfeited.

Dreams may also employ transport metaphors to point towards the realization of our immediate goals. Missing a train, a bus or a plane could signify the fear of losing an opportunity, the anxiety of not being there for an important meeting or feeling that life is passing us by.

> *Having waited for what seemed hours, I turned my back for just a moment and missed the bus I was meant to catch. I ran after it shouting and gesticulating to make it stop but it disappeared down the road in a haze of dust.*

This was 'Meenakshi Sinha's' dream, who, still single at 36, felt she had 'missed the bus'. Her long wait for the bus and then its leaving without her was a metaphor for her dwindling hope of marriage.

Sex

Many people are alarmed by explicit sexual dreams since the subject of sex is overarched by social and moral constraints. These dreams are dominated by overt sexual content and mostly have a singularity of focus. A woman dreamt:

> *I am having sexual intercourse with a stranger in the back of the bus, completely oblivious of the other passengers.*

Frankly, sexual dreams are common to both men and women, especially in adolescence. Although sometimes the sexual content of male dreams is openly manifest in the wet dream, women are equally prone to sexual dreams.[5] One study, for example, found that women's dreams are influenced by the menstrual cycle. They tend to have erotic dreams during the first half of their cycle, when the sex hormone is most active. 'During the second half of the menstrual cycle when the maternal hormone comes to the fore, their dreams become maternal in character.'[6]

Men often feel that erections during sleep are a giveaway of the erotic content of their dreams, but that perhaps is not strictly true. Researchers have discovered that genital arousal during sleep has a physiological explanation.

We already know that certain physiological changes in a sleeping subject can alert laboratory researchers to the onset of a dream. The most prominent being the rapid eye movements and muscular atonia. However, there is one other physical phenomenon that has been observed, recurrently: REM sleep is very strongly connected with genital arousal.

In fact, regardless of the content, every time men experience a dream, they will have an erection.

Often, the 'sex impulse is framed in a larger, more complicated picture, the analysis of which yields considerable knowledge about the dreamer's total conception of sexuality and all of its ramifications in his personality'.[7] If the person conceives of sex as something to be ashamed of, then the dream imagery—like in the sex dream above—will be consonant with this idea. The woman whose dream this is, was surprised that she indulged in the sexual act despite people watching her. If sex is viewed as a dangerous, alien force, like Manish did in chapter 3, it will then appear in his dream as a battle. To take another example, a woman dreamt:

> My school teacher is making passionate love to me in an unhurried way. He gradually builds it up, so that every gesture is an invitation which culminates in a refined eroticism. Slowly, not only our sexual communion, but the whole room is aglow with a marvellous radiance.

Her dream may be indicative of her personal sexual predilections. However, it may not be restricted to that alone. The dream also suggests the discovery of that particular glow which can inform sex, but which goes far beyond the act itself. Jung felt that sexual themes symbolize a higher creative process, as seen in the erotic sculptures that adorn the exteriors of many Hindu temples. They do not refer simply to the sexual union of male and female, but to the wholeness within the Self and to the marriage of opposites—of the earth and sky, mortal and divine, spirit and matter.[8]

Being Naked in Public

Contrary to what is widely believed, dreams of being naked in public have nothing to do with sexuality, but often with feeling exposed, embarrassed or ashamed.[9] They usually allude to some circumstance in the dreamer's life that makes him or her feel stripped of normal defences. Strangely, it is mostly only the dreamer who is aware of his or her nudity—other people in the dream appear to be oblivious to it. Perhaps the dream is cautioning the dreamer that his or her vulnerability is more an internal notion than an external reality.

Clothes, it may be pointed out, can represent our identity. A policeman's clothes are different from a factory worker's, a business executive's from those of a doctor. Clothes can represent not only our occupational status, but also our social status; people are often judged by the clothes they wear. Seeing yourself naked in a dream may thus be a way of asking, 'What will people think of me if they see me for what I really am?' Dreams of nudity could also indicate honesty, where the dreamer stands exposed, open and vulnerable towards another as an expression of trust in the relationship. Also, the discarding of clothes may represent a violation of the social code and indicate the dreamer's desire to rise above social restrictions.

Freud believed that in the innocence of infancy we have no shame in our nakedness. In fact, children love to laugh and jump and slap themselves in their nakedness, enjoying this intoxicating display, which is often met by their mothers' disapproval. He believed that the childhood desire for exhibitionism resurfaces as dreams of nakedness in adulthood—this being an expression of the original infantile self-display that was repressed due to punitive parental attitudes. The censure expresses itself as the distress or shame experienced in the dream. Thus, to Freud, these are also wish-fulfilment dreams.[10]

Teeth Falling Out

The biographers of Emperor Ashoka (third century BCE) tell us that the king dreamt one night of his teeth falling out. He summoned his dream interpreters and asked them what his dream portended. They said:

> One whose teeth decay
> And fall out in a dream
> Will see his son's eyes destroyed
> And the death of his son as well.

Hearing these words, a distressed King Ashoka began making salutations to the deities, imploring them to protect his son Kunala.[11]

The belief that falling teeth are an ominous portent was not only the preserve of Buddhist oneirology, but a view also held by many cultures. The Puranas warn that 'one whose teeth are broken or fallen meets with the loss of wealth besides suffering bodily disease'.[12] In the Talmud, teeth were interpreted as members of the dreamer's family, and death was foretold for a particular member after a dream featuring falling teeth.[13] Artemidorus, a professional diviner who lived in Greece in the second century CE, laid down guidelines on how to distinguish who would die after such a dream: 'The upper teeth represent the more important and excellent members of the dreamer's household; the lower, those less important… Furthermore, the so-called incisor teeth or front teeth signify the young; the canine teeth, the middle-aged; the molars, old people. Therefore the type of person he is to lose is indicated by the type of tooth he loses.'[14]

Modern-day interpreters hold a diametrically opposite view. They argue that since research has indicated this type of dream to be more frequent among women, it refers to giving birth—a small object is expelled from an orifice of the woman's body, resulting in pain and bleeding. This dovetails very neatly with the folk-belief that a woman loses a tooth for every baby she bears.[15] As a rule, Freud would interpret a dream of someone else pulling out a tooth to mean fear of being castrated. Stekel even included dreams of having one's hair cut in this category.[16] The common element in these interpretations is the separation of a part of the body from the whole.

At a symbolic level 'losing teeth' could be alluding to one's inability to 'chew' on a particular experience, finding it hard to grasp or comprehend it. We are toothless at two stages of our life—in infancy and in old age. Both are characterized by helplessness and dependence. 'Losing teeth' could be a concern with aging, the general diminution of one's powers and the attendant feelings of loss of control. Most people who recount dreams of falling teeth feel anxious and distressed in the dream. When asked why they felt anxious, many replied, 'But I looked awful! And how am I supposed to speak without my teeth?' Such unease is often created in the dream from some waking concern that triggered it.

Recurrent Dreams

Most people experience typical dreams at some stage in their life. A recurrent dream, as the term implies, is one that repeats itself again and again. These recurrent dreams may have thematically similar images as in typical dreams of being chased, taking an examination, flying or falling. They could also simply be characterized by the repetition of a symbol, a character or an emotion, for years in some instances. Approximately two-thirds of adults experience some form of repetitive dreams and most of them seem to be associated with stressful events.[17]

Functional efficiency demands that we identify our problems, understand their psychodynamics and resolve them through discursive reasoning. This may not be entirely applicable in life—we do dwell on our problems, often stating and restating them, repeatedly wanting to discuss them over long stretches of time, like a recurrent dream. A close parallel to this is a child's fascination with fairy tales, which parents usually read to them at bedtime. Bruno Bettelheim, who distinguished himself with his psychoanalytic work with children, studied the meaning and importance of fairy tales. In *The Uses of Enchantment*, he wrote, 'Soon he [the child] will indicate that a certain story has become important to him by his immediate response to it, or by his asking to be told this story over and over again.'[18] Bettelheim believes that this repeated interest in a particular fairy tale is the child's attempt to come to terms with 'the psychological problems of growing up—overcoming narcissistic disappointments, oedipal dilemmas, sibling rivalries; becoming able to relinquish childhood dependencies; gaining a feeling of selfhood and of self-worth…'[19] The adventures and final resolution in the fairy tale become the symbolic matrix through which the child imaginatively journeys in the attempt to try and come to terms with the current problem. Similarly, by repeating themselves, dream images draw our attention to an issue that is seeking resolution.

Jung attached great significance to recurrent dreams and believed they were 'of specific importance for the integration of the (overall) psyche',[20] periodically reminding the dreamer that a pending matter awaits settlement. He wrote: 'There are cases in which people have dreamed the same dream from childhood into the later years of adult life. A dream of this kind is usually an attempt to compensate for a particular defect in the dreamer's attitude to life; or it may date from a traumatic moment that has left behind some specific prejudice. It may also sometimes anticipate a future event of importance.'[21]

'Anil Ahuja's' recurrent dream is one such example:

I am fleeing in absolute terror from something that is pursuing me. I cannot even turn around to see what it is. I have to cross a river but as I try to do so, the water turns into thick rubber sheets, which clamp my feet down. I struggle again and again to extricate my feet but cannot, all the while fearing that my pursuer is gaining ground and I will not be able to get away.

If Anil had dreamt this once or twice, we may have treated it as an anxiety dream of being chased. The sheer repetition of the dream over many years alerts our attention to something more powerful and significant. The dominant metaphor is the feeling of being stuck. The dreamer appears to be escaping his pursuer (the challenge) but is unexpectedly hampered midway through the river.

And curiously enough Anil had tried his hand at many things without feeling successful at anything. He had a degree in Fine Arts from Paris, but had not painted for the past twenty years. He had tried his hand at rural education, but then switched to handicrafts. Later, he attempted to write a book. When he related this dream to me, his current business enterprise, a modest one, was facing the threat of closure, and he and his partner had fallen out with each other. Anil was convinced that every project he undertook was doomed to remain unsuccessful. Chased by the demons of frustration, he felt paralysed, unable to progress in any venture he undertook. He found himself trapped in a repetitive cycle of failure.

Not all recurrent dreams have an anxiety theme like that of Anil's though. Some have a much more frightening content, and these have the potential for becoming nightmares.

5. Nightmares: Terrors of the Dreaming World

Nightmares are typically associated with an overwhelming state of anxiety which often awakens the dreamer. They are very different from the anxiety dreams we have been discussing till now. We may label them as 'bad dreams'. Researchers have distinguished among a variety of experiences, including night terrors, that are generally referred to as nightmares.

Almost everyone has had a nightmare at some point in their life, most likely in childhood. Some are so powerful that they are vividly remembered throughout our lives. Statistically, nightmares commonly occur between the ages of three and six. While they become less frequent after the age of six, their incidence may increase again in adolescence between the ages of thirteen and eighteen.[1]

Ernest Hartmann, the director of a sleep laboratory at Lemuel Shattuck Hospital in Boston, has extensively researched nightmares. He believes that average nightmare-sufferers have certain personality features that make them prone to such dreams. Typically, they have an open personality, and are easily hurt, self-disclosing and vulnerable. He characterizes them as having 'thin boundaries' so that they often merge thought and feelings and sometimes have vivid fantasies that are difficult to distinguish from reality.[2] Research also suggests that people in the arts or other creative pursuits are more prone to nightmares than the blue- or white-collared worker.[3]

Living through the coronavirus pandemic, many people experienced nightmares in line with symptoms of post-traumatic disorders. A report in the *National Geographic* issue of April 15, 2020, cites research on pandemic dreams collated in March 2020. Among the participants were healthcare workers, those affected by the disease and those confined and isolated. Some participants dreamt of having caught the virus, or dying of it. Most participants found pandemic dreams frightening and weird.

Nightmares are relatively rare for adults. In a child, REM sleep may be more intense and their imagination more vivid too. This may lead to higher levels of fear or confusion in some of their dreams. Maybe that is the reason why nightmares are less common in adults.

Daytime events and feelings that trigger nightmares and bad dreams are often linked to some deep fear, frustration or resentment, which may be a lifelong trouble spot that the dreamer has avoided confronting. Such dreams may then serve the very useful function of turning the spotlight on the ignored problem and pointing to its source. It helps the dreamer take the first significant step to resolving it. The Senoi method of facing the danger in the dream and then conquering it consciously can be useful in dealing with nightmares.

Not all nightmares originate in psychological causes; physiological issues too may provoke them at times. However, the physical disorder merely sets off the dream.

The dream imagery is determined by the psychological condition of the dreamer. Hartmann describes several physiological causes of nightmares, the most common being drug-related as some forms of medication are known to trigger them.[4] If you suddenly begin to have frequent nightmares for the first time in your life, your first step should be to consult your doctor.

Night Terrors

The difference between a nightmare and a night terror is that there is a very detailed recall of the dream events in the former, while the latter often leaves people with a short, single frightening image, for example, of being choked or crushed. A scream frequently precedes awakening from a night terror, and is followed by temporary disorientation. Clinically, a nightmare is associated with the later rounds of REM sleep, usually early morning. A night terror, on the other hand, occurs during the first two hours of sleep and is associated with NREM Stage 4 of the sleep cycle.[5]

Night terrors, like nightmares, are most common in children. Their frequency decreases as the child grows older. Many researchers are hesitant to refer to night terrors as genuine dreams. Rather than see them as an attempt of the unconscious to highlight psychological conflicts (as in a nightmare), they ascribe them to the effect of sudden shifts in the physiological status of the body during sleep. In a night terror, tremendous changes in the autonomic nervous system take place very rapidly—the pulse and respiratory rates sometimes double in the process. As the awakening is abrupt and involves such dramatic shifts in the nervous system, night terrors have been classified as 'disorders of arousal'.[6] Sleepwalking sometimes follows the onset of a night terror. Unlike nightmares—where a symbolic dream narrative is being unfolded that gradually awakens the sleeper—in a night terror, the awakening is very abrupt with no recollection of the dream.

Post-trauma Dreams

Post-traumatic dreams replay traumatic events of our life—or variants of them, over and over again—such as combat scenes, assault, natural calamities, accidents and a loss that the dreamer may have been unfortunate enough to experience. These are a mixture of nightmares and night terrors—they can occur both during NREM sleep, when night terrors usually occur, and during REM sleep, when most ordinary nightmares arise.[7]

Traumatic experiences usually leave a scar on the psyche, which may be reflected in dreams. Almost every traumatized individual experiences some kind of nightmare, incorporating the trauma. After a severe accident, a fire or the death of someone close, dreams may continue to reflect this in one way or another for a few weeks. However, for some individuals these continue to recur over many years. Clinical researchers do not tend to treat this at the level of an 'ordinary' nightmare. Hartmann and others, after studying veterans of the Vietnam War, treat them as 'memory intrusions' into dreams.[8]

Wars can inflict tremendous devastation, but their cost in human terms—the scars carried by the survivors, the personal hells they live through in their private worlds at night—is rarely discussed or understood. During the Second World War, in January 1943, marine engineer

Ramesh Khanna was on a merchant ship off the Cape of Good Hope, near Durban, when a German submarine torpedoed his ship. He jumped into the water and scrambled onto a lifeboat. More and more survivors got onto the boat till it could hold no more, and it sank. Ramesh soon found a lifebuoy and clutched onto it, but so did ten others. Predictably, it also sank, and Ramesh had to keep afloat unaided. Sixteen hours elapsed before he was picked up by an Allied warship. He was hospitalized for three months in Durban, and heavily tranquillized to enable him to come to terms with the trauma. He was a courageous man. Before the end of the year, he was back to sailing again on another merchant vessel. History repeated itself in 1944 when his ship was sunk once again, this time in the Pacific Ocean. After recuperating, he still continued to sail. He, however, was prescribed mild sedatives every night to protect him from his trauma.

After the war, he was travelling home on leave from Mumbai to Lahore on the Peshawar Frontier Mail train when his traumatic memory intruded his sleep. He was sleeping on the upper berth of a first-class compartment. While fast asleep, he jumped down and leapt for the door, ready to jump out of the moving train as though it was a sinking ship. Luckily, the person sleeping on the lower berth held on to Ramesh before he could jump off the train. The gentle rocking of the train must have rekindled Ramesh Khanna's memory of being on a rolling ship. Perhaps a jerk of the train had triggered his memory of being torpedoed. He instinctively lunged for the door to bail out. For many years afterwards, he needed to be protected from this intrusion of memory by ensuring that someone travelled with him, just in case. With the passage of time the intensity of the trauma gradually diminished, but not without the help of sedatives, which he continued to take for many years.

We've noted earlier how during dream (REM) sleep the muscular tonus is reduced, foreclosing the option of movement while dreaming. Ramesh Khanna did exercise muscular control in jumping down and opening the door, probably indicating that his *memory intrusion* was not experienced during REM sleep, but during non-dreaming or NREM sleep.

An 'ordinary' nightmare or a bad dream tries to highlight a fear, or a conflict, in its attempt to absorb it. The unconscious tries to heal the wound, by presenting it in various forms for it to be wholly accepted or ingested. However, the post-traumatic-repetitive nightmare sometimes fails to do this. The unabsorbed traumatic material continues to haunt the dreamer's psyche. Hartmann says, 'It is branded or etched into memory. It is "encapsulated" somewhat like an abscess, separated by a wall and yet tender to touch.'[9]

~

So far, our attempt has been to 'Explain all that', as the Mock Turtle says, in *Alice's Adventures in Wonderland*. We have looked at various types of dreams, what the scientific world thinks of them, and whether they have meaning. I have also tried to fashion a simple method by which each person can 'explain' their dreams to themselves.

But it's now time to heed the Gryphon who impatiently declared: 'No, no! The adventures first! Explanations take such a dreadful time.'

6. Choices, the Hinges of Destiny

Kavita Nayar, an established Delhi-based painter whose work has been exhibited in many countries, recounted a powerful dream that she had more than sixteen years ago. We sat in the living room of her three-bedroom apartment-cum-studio. Everything in the house diminished, receded, in the overwhelming presence of the paintings that met you on the walls, in the corridor, stacked outside the kitchen, in one of the bedrooms. Opposite where I sat was one of a pensive woman sitting on a windowsill; in another, a woman appeared walking away into the distance, her red scarf swelled by the wind. In yet another painting, the trunk of a tree transformed into a hand reaching for the sky. These canvases seemed to be exploring human aloneness.

'Sixteen years ago, a single dream changed everything for me,' Kavita said.

'That's a long time to hold the memory of a dream,' I commented. Kavita was lost in thought.

'What was the dream?' I asked.

In front of Society Cinema in Kolkata there is a pavement temple with zigzag black and white marble flooring. Instead of the image of Kali in it, there stands the figure of Shiva. I have to cross the street and get to this temple but I'm unable to do that. I stand rooted at the edge of the street with tears flowing down my cheeks as I cannot cross the road. Suddenly the image of Shiva comes to life as he beckons me to cross the road and come to him. I protest by saying, 'How can I cross? Hanuman is lying across the road.'

To my surprise Hanuman gets up and moves away, saying, 'Go, the path is clear.'

I look up, only to see Shiva smiling, and he says, 'Cross, and it will be all right.'

I take my first step towards him.

The simple act of crossing the road has filled Kavita with so much anguish. She is weeping, unable to cross. Crossing is a metaphor for choosing, taking a decisive step, leaving something behind. What is stopping her?

I looked towards her. 'Which road could you not cross?'

Kavita smiled.

Had I looked more closely, I'd have recognized two powerful symbols that are part of the story—Shiva, the erotic ascetic god, and Hanuman, the bachelor god and teacher of celibacy. Did the issue pertain to marrying or remaining single? But Hanuman, according to Kavita, removes obstacles, and Shiva is also beckoning her to cross. Clearly, Kavita was unsure which road was hers to take.

There are periods in life when a single issue or conflict dominates the landscape of the mind for months, maybe years. At such points a dream may emerge from the profound depths of the psyche compelling us towards a particular path that is meant for us. Typically, figures appear in such dreams that stir up emotions not ordinarily experienced in everyday life, symbolically portraying a truth that has no conscious equivalent. It is not unusual to see gods and goddesses or mythological figures in these dreams, which leave the dreamer feeling that wisdom from a transpersonal source has been received.

Are we to assume then that a god or goddess, a holy person or a guru appearing in a dream augurs well for the dreamer? Mythic figures, in themselves, contain no moral judgement of 'good' or 'bad', no aesthetic pronouncements of 'beautiful' or 'ugly'.

Lord Shiva appeared in another dream, this time in a young girl's who was ready for marriage. 'Megha' was eighteen when she met 'Suresh', a man who personified all she desired—talent, good looks—and he was a successful businessman. On the night of her engagement, she dreamt:

> *Lord Shiva is sitting cross-legged, opposite me. I see him with his hair in a coil of matted locks, adorned with the crescent moon, and a trident in one hand. I am overwhelmed by his presence and bow my head. He asks me to extend my hand. When I do so he places a small but heavy object wrapped in a red cloth into my outstretched hand. Lord Shiva says somewhat sternly: 'Do not open it till I tell you to.' But I am so overwhelmed with curiosity that I open it. Much to my delight it is a gold necklace, which I promptly wear around my neck.*

Despite Shiva's dream injunction, Megha felt justified in opening the bundle. After she saw the gold necklace, it confirmed her belief that fortune was on her side.

Unfortunately, her fairy tale ended soon after the wedding. The 'most eligible bachelor' turned out to be a narcissistic womanizer, who, without remorse, flaunted his numerous affairs in her face.

Only in retrospect did she realize that the lead metaphor in the dream—the injunction not to open the gift—was a warning and not a blessing. Shiva is cautioning her to leave Suresh alone. For her, the whole issue was so imbued with desire—symbolized by the gift being wrapped in a red cloth—that she ignored the warning and opened it. The gold necklace was a symbol of the Shakespearean warning. 'All that glisters is not gold... Gilded tombs do worms enfold...' Megha quoted, forlornly.

Was the god who appeared to the love-struck Megha an apocryphal figure? The outcome of her dream was very different than Kavita's, though both had dreamt of the same god. Perhaps the difference was in the instructions given by the god in the two cases.

These are archetypal dreams, or what Jung called 'big' dreams. These dreams not only address a personal dilemma but also transcend it, signifying an important transition point where a critical choice has to be exercised.

To return to Kavita's cross-roads...

'You had struggled long enough with a conflict that defied any solution. But did your dream suggest a way?' I asked Kavita.

'The power of the dream was such that I felt assured, at a much deeper level, about the choice I had to make. You see, my personal situation had become so charged that, after the dream, I felt a sense of relief, a handing over of a burden,' Kavita said, her large eyes softening with remembrance.

'Were you in love but were being forced into marrying someone else?'

'Not at all. If I were, it would have resolved the issue. Marriage itself did not hold any attraction for me.'

The conflict in Kavita's life arose between her all-consuming passion to paint and her parents' view that it was but an escape from the demands of marriage.

Since childhood, Kavita had felt the need to paint. Her parents wanted her to study the Sciences, her mother constantly reminding her that painting at best could but be a hobby for a well-brought-up girl, never a profession.

In the course of our conversation Kavita recounted two earlier dreams. She was about sixteen when she had this dream:

> *I am standing on the terrace of my house. Everything around me is being bombarded, razed to the ground. No neighbouring house remains, no maidan, no buildings. I realize that only my house has remained intact in all this debris.*

Years later, Kavita and I tried to unravel this dream in the context of her adult life. At first glance the dream seems only to reflect the reality of her situation. Her resolve to paint had razed everything around her. All that mattered was her vocation even if it meant being isolated. However, a deeper look at the dream suggested it was posing a question that the teenaged Kavita may not have appreciated. Ironically, it seemed to be asking: If you 'bombard' everything around you, how can your art flourish? What the artist expresses cannot be independent of the world. The ambiguities of experience often become the soil in which creativity grows.

When she entered her twenties, her parents began to put pressure on her to get married. She remained resistant, fearing that no man would be able to understand her passion to paint, and she would inevitably be suffocated by the demands of domesticity. If her own parents could not understand its importance, how could a complete stranger do so?

The conflict with her parents came to a head when one morning she found out that a prospective husband, yet another stranger, was being thrust on her.

'You do remember that Pawan and his parents are coming for tea? Please be back on time,' her mother said peremptorily as Kavita was about to leave the house.

With a dull sense of dread, Kavita left for Garhi, the artists' colony where she worked. She wondered how many times she would have to go through this charade before her defences crumbled and she submitted to a decision she would live to regret for the rest of her life.

Kavita worked peacefully all day, but as the shadows of dusk lengthened, laying claim to the day, her thoughts swung back to Pawan and his parents awaiting her arrival at home. She lingered on, delaying the inevitable meeting.

Kavita arrived home in a pigment-stained khadi kurta-pyjama and rubber slippers, trying to look as unappealing as possible. She had hoped that, tired of waiting, Pawan and his parents would have left by the time she returned. But fate would not have it so—the guests were delayed and had arrived only minutes before Kavita did.

'You must have liked him,' her mother asked eagerly after they left. 'He's tall, good-looking and has a very good job.'

Her mother's criteria for a suitable groom always amazed her. If once, only once, she would say, 'You know, this man might support your art.'

On the last such occasion, during her third year at university in Shantiniketan near Kolkata, Kavita's father had arrived with a prospective bridegroom ambling two steps behind him. He took her aside and in a hushed voice told her about the boy, his eyes gleaming in anticipation at the prospect of such a good match.

The flare of anger in her eyes was her only reply. After a while her anger subsided, replaced by a weary acceptance of the inevitable. She got engaged, but without the slightest inclination to get to know her fiancé. He wrote her long letters of love and longing, provoking the only emotion Kavita could muster—that of distant disdain.

She always blamed her phoney engagement for what befell her work at Shantiniketan. Suddenly the full flow of her creative stream just dried up. There was a silence, a blanketing fog that she could not penetrate.

Around this time, she had another dream, which also lingers in her memory:

I am travelling in a bus that meets with an accident. In the accident I lose my left arm. Panic-stricken, I frantically begin to search for it in the mass of bodies strewn on the road. Some are dead, and others are dying, as I pick my way through, searching for my lost left arm. I finally find it and go to a local village doctor and ask him to stitch it back. He stitches it back but it falls off. I then go back and ask him to stick it with Fevicol. He does that.

In hindsight, the central metaphor is the loss of or amputation of a limb. It suggests that something in her life has been severed and she may be feeling 'cut off'. Both the earlier dream and this one have the same background of destruction. Previously, buildings were razed to the ground while in this dream human beings lie injured or dying all around. There is a movement from inanimate objects to human beings, that is, from her external environment to something within her. In spite of this apparent progression, the earlier problem still remains unaccepted or unresolved. The acute anxiety in the second dream conveys this. For Kavita, 'right' signifies the accepted way, the mainstream, the reasoned approach, because the majority of people are right-handed. For her 'left' is where the heart is, the centre of emotions and affections, from where arises the capacity for sympathy, courage, spiritedness and enthusiasm. With the loss of her left arm could she be feeling severed from these positive emotions?

The dream follows three metaphorical sequences: loss, search and renewal. The metaphor of loss only mirrors her predicament, while the second metaphor is asking her to recover from the loss. Only then can renewal take place.

The second metaphor in the current dream finds Kavita going to a village doctor, a man who represents a traditional form of healing. He sticks her arm on, but it falls off. This may be understood in two ways. One, that a conventional, role-oriented approach of relating to her own emotions may not work for her. An attempt to 'stitch' her feelings (arm) in the conventional way results in the arm dropping off. So, she tries another method. She asks the village doctor to stick her arm back with

Fevicol, a brand of adhesive generally used for gluing wood. Naturally, it cannot bind living tissue. Could the dream be suggesting that the engagement was bound to break? At another level, it may also have meant an amputation of her emotions. The dream could be suggesting that Kavita, having severed emotions (left hand) from her life (body), is now resorting to a patchwork of solutions. These do not deal adequately with the loss of emotional flow in her life; an inappropriate quick-fix (glue) is being used, instead of a more relevant 'solution'.

The dream was suggesting something quite contrary to what Kavita was feeling at the time. She believed that her engagement was what caused the drying up of her creative impulses. The dream was telling her otherwise: that this 'drying up' was due to her persistent emotional isolation from others and herself.

However, following her conscious intent to its conclusion, Kavita moved to Delhi after she graduated from Shantiniketan and began to share a flat with a friend. Shocked by such unconventional behaviour, Kavita's fiancé's parents started to whisper among themselves. If their future daughter-in-law could take such a 'bold' step before marriage, how many more independent steps was she capable of taking after she got married? She did not seem the homely, submissive creature they had hoped for. Kavita's fiancé tried to dissuade her from living independently in Delhi, but Kavita ignored his protestations. The engagement was called off. In sheer relief, Kavita wept.

On that occasion destiny had intervened, but now, presented with a new man, Pawan, Kavita felt she would have to tackle the situation herself. She would have to take strong measures to stop Pawan from marrying her, so she asked to meet him alone. Kavita's parents were overjoyed since this was the first time she had taken the initiative to meet any of the young men they had suggested.

Pawan and Kavita met the following evening in a restaurant. She came straight to the point: 'I must tell you from the start that painting is my life, and everything else is secondary to it. I may never earn anything from my paintings and yet I expect my future husband to support all the expenses my art demands. Besides which I will need a studio to work in.'

Pawan kept silent.

'I doubt if you know that I've already broken one engagement, and the fault was mine.'

Pawan stared at her, but still kept silent.

Kavita felt her plan was working. She would push him into rejecting her.

Finally, Pawan asked, 'Were you emotionally involved with this man?'

'Not at all. That was the crux of the problem. I felt nothing for him.' Left unsaid, hanging in the air was the next sentence: *And, if I'm engaged to you, I'll feel nothing for you either.*

More silence ensued as he tried to digest what she said.

'Also, I do not want children for a very long time. In fact, I may not want any of my own but, instead, I might adopt a child.' Kavita had played her trump card, which she thought would daunt every traditional man.

Pawan looked at her with pensive eyes. He realized she was on edge. Instead of reacting to her declarations of war,' he gently asked, 'This desire to paint...has it been with you from very early on?'

Kavita was nonplussed. She had not expected him to come up with a question like this. 'I think I felt its first stirrings when I was eight. Over the years it just grew, till it became the only thing I wanted to do.'

'And you feel marriage will come in the way?' Pawan probed.

'How did you know?'

'From the word go you've done nothing but dissuade me from marrying you.'

Kavita laughed and then looked at Pawan as though for the first time. 'I must match your perception with honesty. I do not want to get married. I'm just being pushed into it all the time.'

'Are you involved with any other man?'

'Oh, God! No!' Kavita said sincerely.

'Have you ever thought that your husband could be proud of you and may want to support what you are doing?'

'I don't live in a dream, Pawan. Very few men would understand the long hours I need to be totally alone to paint. In those moments the world does not exist. What will happen to the simple daily chores—buying vegetables, getting food on the table, mending buttons? Which man could tolerate that?'

'Artists do marry. They manage.'

'But I must feel the need to marry. If that is absent, I'm being unfair to myself and to the other person.'

Two days later Pawan's parents rang up to say that Pawan wished to marry Kavita. Kavita was stunned. What was wrong with the man? Hadn't she told him in plain

English that she did not want to marry? Her parents were overjoyed. Her father would never entertain a 'no' from her now. She was trapped.

A deep depression swept over Kavita. Like the fading light of day, she felt the darkness of domesticity engulfing her. Just to get away she went to Shantiniketan. There she had the dream that changed the course of her life.

For Kavita, Shiva's appearance in the dream was not the symbolic appearance of an archetypal image, emerging from the collective unconscious as Jungian dream theory holds. In any case, she was unfamiliar with Jung's theory. For Kavita, she had actually been graced with Shiva's presence—for her the dream did not need interpretation. It was a message from the gods: go ahead and marry and all will be well. Both Shiva and Hanuman would bless the union.

Jungian theory is right when it says that dreams of numinous figures and gods do not represent mundane answers but are attempts at the reconciliation of opposites that defy resolution to the waking mind. Kavita's single-mindedness with regard to her art would not admit any space for marriage. Yet, as her previous two dreams had hinted, her art and her sense of self stood divorced from all 'others'—all relationships.

Kavita felt that this dream was a turning point for her. She returned to Delhi and found herself phoning Pawan without knowing why or what to say to him. All she did was to narrate her dream as though it was her answer to him.

Kavita married Pawan, who not only grew to appreciate her art but also actively supported her work, even though they lived in a joint family. Though Pawan himself had never been exposed to painting, music or the arts, he accompanied Kavita to art exhibitions and concerts late in the evenings, always willing to learn.

By the time I met Kavita, she had created more than 500 individual works. In fact, her work could be classified into four distinct stages: beginning with the *Me Alone* series depicting the primal state of loneliness, followed by the *You and Me* series, where loneliness is partially offset by the presence of the other, and more fully offset in the *We Together* series, where emotional union is achieved, to the crescendo of the *Entwined* series which celebrates the joys of union. A progression depicted through her dreams. Fittingly, art critic Suneet Chopra commented in *The Economic Times*: 'It is interesting to observe how Kavita has moved from expressing feelings of alienation to reaching out and evoking relationships and harmonizing them with an environment that has been domesticated yet has a life of its own. This is essentially different from the existentialist position of being the outsider looking in.'

Perhaps Kavita had actually found 'love'. And her dreams helped her settle for nothing less.

~

One small question remains. How did the dreaming intelligence know in advance what was right for the dreamer? That Kavita should marry and Megha should not—are these choices predetermined? Is destiny intervening directly through dreams or merely revealing it? Or is it that when the dreamer is strongly disturbed or intensely desirous of a particular outcome our interpretation tilts in that direction? For Megha, the issue was imbued with desire (symbolized by the red cloth) compelling her to disregard Shiva's words and open the gift to marry Suresh and be confronted with the consequences of her choice. Myths and folk tales abound with stories of how when a command given by a god or goddess is disobeyed, it leads to pain and suffering, as, for example, in the biblical story of Adam and Eve.

~

The next dream I wish to share is about a very different kind of choice. 'Akanksha', married with two children and settled abroad, was nearing her mid-life crisis when she had an impactful dream:

> I have to go up in the lift to the fourteenth floor. Finally, two lifts come down together, and their doors open. One lift, to my left, is large and spacious. The other is tiny and is actually an Indian style toilet, an untidy but clean one, with a frayed green carpet. I step into the toilet lift instead of the larger one. I don't know why it is so clear to me that I had to choose the toilet lift. Then as soon as I do, I regret it. As it goes up, the door doesn't open. I keep waiting but it refuses to open. I'm terrified.

An interpretational dilemma faces us here. It focuses on a choice, quite unlike the choices presented to Kavita and Megha but a choice that had been made already. In the dream she chooses the toilet lift against all good sense and reason. She must have been bound by a strange compulsion that prevents her from stepping into the more comfortable lift. What is this 'choice' that the dream is alluding to? The clue may be sought in the number fourteen, which Akanksha had associated with the number of years she had been married, a direct allusion to her 'choice' of 'Abhishek' as her life partner.

Like the toilet lift, is her life with Abhishek at this point of time feeling cramped, isolating and restrictive? The dream also suggests that she cannot get out of the lift. She is gripped with terror, but the door of the lift does not open to let her out. However difficult her relationship with Abhishek has become, something prevents her from opting out. How may we understand her choices?

None of us choose or opt for difficulties and reversals. They seem to just happen as part of the course of life. Yet in Akanksha's dream there is an awareness of deliberately making a choice that spelt difficult life circumstances. Two lifts came down. Two sets of opportunities were presented to her. One a large, spacious, comfortable one and the other a cramped Indian-style toilet lift, symbolizing restriction and difficulties. She notes the difference in the travelling conditions of the two lifts, yet opts for the more uncomfortable one. Something utterly mysterious is operating here. The minute we perceive that a choice spells discomfort we generally avoid it. But Akanksha did not.

Was she locked in because of predestination?

If her life is fated, if her choice of marrying Abhishek is predetermined, then why struggle to understand her conflict or set on the path of personal individuation? Just accept the fated event, follow the traditional approach, and abandon any hopes for change. Stated this way, the dream appears meaningless.

To succumb to the temptation of saying that her 'choice' of Abhishek as life partner—an option she had exercised fourteen years ago—is the central issue in the dream would further reduce the import of the dream. Nor can we say that in casting a backward glance Akanksha is regretting her present option. More likely the dream seemed to affirm that had she known the difficulties, she may still have chosen the cramped lift—a turbulent life with Abhishek.

We can only conjecture that some deeper force was at work, a purposive thrust that could operate only through her choice of the cramped lift. She 'needed' to choose that lift to fulfil her real purpose in life. We can only guess what that purpose is, but can never really be sure. Broadening the scope of Akanksha's dream, we can but hypothesize that the psyche in its wisdom chooses circumstances that may not necessarily be commodious and agreeable, but are perceived as essential for its development towards higher octaves of self-understanding.

The toilet lift may give us a clue about what Akanksha has chosen to learn. In an Indian-style toilet the process of elimination is often faster because one is squatting uncomfortably on one's haunches, unlike the chair-like comfort of a Western toilet seat. Could it be that Akanksha chose the toilet lift because it would perhaps help her eliminate expendable psychic baggage faster? Akanksha later told me that this phase of her life had transformed her, and had pushed her into seeking meaning at an internal level. In this evolution, she had to shed or eliminate what was toxic, wasteful and redundant in terms of emotional baggage—her sense of injustice, acute resentments, unbridled fear and chronic anxieties. Like Psyche's first painstaking task of sorting seeds in the Greek myth, she had to sort and separate the emotions to discern the meaning of her tribulations. In coping with these emotions she discovered a new strength. Was this the lesson she had chosen to learn, and as her dreams pointed out, was capable of learning?

~

Sometimes the real-life choices our dreams are pushing us towards can be much harder to grasp.

The disaster that 'Geeta Prasher' was heading towards seemed to be an emotional one. Her marriage, eaten away by incompatibility, had left her with a hollow echo sounding within the empty corridors of parallel lives—her own and that of her husband. Then one night she dreamt:

> I see my husband going to someone's house. He rings the bell and a woman opens the door. They embrace each other as lovers would. I cannot see the woman's face but I realize she is someone I know very well. I'm struck by the fact that my husband knows this woman through me.

Geeta could not figure out her dream's suggestion. Only after a month-and-a-half, when she unexpectedly went over to her closest friend's house, did she realize who the woman was. It was her best friend, and she was in her husband's arms. In one shattering moment she lived through dream and reality simultaneously. The dream was actually a warning.

No doubt many an anxious husband or wife may dream of their spouse's infidelity. And, of course, every anxiety dream is far from being a warning dream. Yet despite the vividness of the dream and its tenacity, Geeta had ignored the possibility of it being a warning. Most dreams dissolve like mist, evaporating when the dreamer awakens. This dream continued to plague her long after it occurred and may have ultimately led to her exercising a choice about her marriage.

A similar insistent quality in a later dream alerted Geeta to another change in her life. The affair between her husband and her friend continued, despite Geeta's violent protests. Crushed by her husband's remorseless infidelity, she decided to move out of the house with her two children—making the painful choice of separating but not divorcing her husband, a choice many women in a similar situation are forced to make. Her friend and her husband began living together and a year later announced their intention of getting married. Two months after learning of this news she had another dream:

> *A preparation for a marriage is underway. I see my friend dressed in bridal clothes, getting ready to marry my estranged husband. Relatives from both sides are laughing and singing as they wait for the bridegroom to appear. I am going from one relative to another saying, 'He will not turn up for the wedding. He's not going to come, believe me.' No one listens to me—it is as though I'm invisible. I'm like a ghost who feels the reality of its own presence and thoughts, without anyone else relating to it.*

The dream could be read as Geeta's intense wish to stop the wedding by convincing herself that the bridegroom was unwilling to marry, or, contrary to the news of the forthcoming wedding, the dream was predicting an unexpected end to the affair. Simultaneously, her decision to not divorce her husband had confronted her with another choice. Soon afterwards, her estranged husband called her to say he was not marrying her friend; they had parted ways for good. He asked Geeta if she would consider allowing him back in her life.

May we then say that when we stand on the cusp of choice the wheels of destiny come into motion, nudging us through dreams towards a path meant for us? But the greater mystery that confronts us is: Do dreams reveal destiny, a seeming predetermined event, in which we still seem to have the elasticity of choice?

7. If Love Is the Answer, What May Be the Question?

At a family gathering, my twenty-three-year-old nephew hesitatingly asked me, 'What kinds of dreams are most common at my age group?'

'Sexual.'

'Ah!' he sighed with relief. 'And at what age do they stop?'

'Never. Only their frequency gets reduced.'

'You mean granny may still have…' he left the sentence incomplete, balking at the thought.

'Dreams can be frankly sexual, or indirectly so,' I said.

'Indirectly sexual? As in…'

He looked up, puzzled. I smiled. Little did he realize that I was voicing Freud's dictum that all dreams are sexual but their content is disguised.

'For example, a man dreamt he was bicycling with his neighbours "Vikram" and "Anjali" to a picnic lunch. But Anjali's cycle doesn't have enough air. Before setting off, he quickly pumps the tyre.

'It seems a trivial, mundane dream. But Freud would have read that the dreamer desired Anjali. This forbidden urge was disguised, and replaced with a harmless image of pumping her bicycle tyre. According to Freud most dream images are symbolic of sexual content: anything which is longer than it is broad represents the phallus, circular objects stand for the vagina, and climbing stairs, riding a horse or pumping a bicycle tyre are symbolic of the sexual act. The dream expresses his desire, yet disguises its potency. You see now what indirect sexual content is?'

Awkwardly, he asked, 'Can I share my friend's dream? A frankly sexual one.'

'But of course.' I wondered if the dream was actually his own.

He handed a typed sheet to me. He must have planned this quite meticulously, I thought. It must be really bothering him. My heart went out to him. I read the dream.

My family had just finished eating dinner at home. The two girls, aged between five and seven years old, ran up the stairs in their pyjamas and pigtails to get ready for bed. My wife was sitting at the kitchen table reading a magazine. I was happily collecting the dishes to wash. The downstairs looked very similar to my parents' house, but cosier and more approachable due to some art projects and paperwork from the girls. When I turned on the water, I turned into a middle-aged, balding, overweight man. But naked and with a three-foot-long completely erect penis. I call to my wife, 'Honey, it's happening again...' I wasn't particularly mad that it had happened. My attitude was more 'it is what it is'. She sighs and gets up from the kitchen table to start sucking my incredulously long dick. I have both hands on my hips as she is doing so. She is only able to at most get halfway up at full size. I start morphing back to my feminine self with the continued help of my wife. I hear footsteps coming down the stairs. 'Excuse me...' says a sweet voice from one of the little girls. 'Not now, sweeties. Go back to bed. I'll be right up.'

At first glance the dream seemed to be about his performance anxiety; he feared he was as attractive as a balding, overweight, middle-aged man. However, this is compensated by an extraordinarily long penis.

I tried to assure him. 'There is nothing unusual in this dream. Most men worry if they will be able to perform satisfactorily. Do you think middle-aged men are sexually over the hill?' I tried not to smile or look at the 'uncles' in the room.

He looked down at his sneakers. There was further precarious territory to traverse. The dream was set in the parental house, but it was 'cosier and more approachable'. Did the talk of sexuality in front of his parents make him uncomfortable? A common enough situation. Perhaps it was reflective of the transition in urban India's mindset where family norms were the precedent for social behaviour. The relaxation of social and sexual barriers, an easier intermingling of the sexes, access to contraception and the exploration of romantic love versus arranged marriages upset the norm. Dressed to show skin in hip-hugging jeans and snug tank tops, youngsters are courting love over coffee and movie dates and exploring live-in relationships. On the other hand, they do not protest when parents wish to marry them according to caste and astrology. Naturally, sex cannot be a 'cosy' subject in the parental home. But this was *my* nephew. I had always considered *my* family to be 'modern'. The dream made me ask: are we really?

The puzzling part of the dream, however, was that he was 'morphing back to [his] feminine self'. Was my nephew dealing with gender confusion? I looked at him anew. Long hair, tied in a ponytail, a T-shirt, two sizes too small, clung to his chest, his eyes sparkled with mischief. As an example of male machismo, he drove his Scorpio at near-death-experience speed, and had even brought home a girlfriend once.

Each of us has both male and female aspects. When one aspect is more overt than the other, it determines our psychological sex. Was the overt part being compensated in his dream by highlighting the neglected, passive aspect of his nature?

Keeping up the charade, I asked, 'Is your friend going through some emotional upheaval with his girlfriend?'

'My friend is a woman!'

I was stunned! I had missed the clue—the dreamer had *morphed back into her feminine self*. Not only was it not my nephew's dream, it wasn't even a man's dream!

'The only masculine thing about "Rosie" is that she is 5 feet 10 inches tall.'

Recovering from my shock, I asked, 'Was she often compared to her male peers?'

'Very much so. But she is straight. She definitely is not transgender either. She's just out of a two-year relationship with a man.'

Then what is Rosie's dream about? My mind went straight towards penis envy. Freud postulated that it originates in the girl child's discovery of anatomical differences between her and a boy, and it leads to her feeling deprived. Could that be why Rosie is a man in the dream? Did Rosie believe that if she had a brother, she would be lesser than him, and is that why she is proudly announcing in the dream, '*Honey, it's happening again*'? Girls, according to Freud, assume that they previously possessed a penis but lost it by castration. Is this why Rosie is dreaming of having a penis, and a pretty big one too, as if to compensate for the loss? The dream also depicts the girl's wish to acquire a penis by swallowing it. Somehow, even though all this neatly dovetailed with Freud's theory, I wasn't satisfied. It was a complex dream and it must have been touching upon other dimensions of Rosie's life.

I began a correspondence with Rosie to find out more about her and the dream. She willingly responded. To my query about her dream home appearing cosier and more approachable, she wrote back, 'I remember spending most of my creative time during childhood in my bedroom (that I shared with my sister, two years younger than me) and sometimes the game room, but never the downstairs area (where the dream takes place) as that was my mother's area. Often, when friends came over, they would comment that the downstairs looked creepy because it was too clean and looked like nobody lived there.'

I then asked her: Was there some encounter with a middle-aged man who turned antagonistic towards you? Did it happen around the age of five and seven (the age of the two girls in the dream)? Usually numbers in a dream often mark milestones of forgotten events that are still potent. Also, if other people are present during lovemaking, then it is important to explore who these people are. Our images of parents, siblings, rivals or other lovers vastly complicate our view of the sexual act.

She wrote: 'Only since you asked I remembered that this happened. Between the ages of five and seven, there was one time when I went to church with just my dad. As we were sitting in the pew (I was sitting like my dad with my legs spread apart) and listening to the sermon, my dad whispered to me to close my legs because a man "over there" was staring at me because of how I sat. I was not able to see the man. Of course, I was freaked out and I didn't understand why we *had* to sit in different ways until much later.'

Was the dream highlighting her sense of shame? It had happened in a church, a setting where it was natural to feel she had 'sinned'. Much later, Rosie did realize the 'why' of the shame, but by then a natural drive had been converted into a demon, leading to Rosie feeling unattractive as a woman, and perhaps unable to own her sexuality. Did she later oscillate between a 'sweet feminine voice' (symbolized by one of the girls) trying to own her femininity, and a wish to be a powerful, virile male, being serviced by a woman, instead of having to serve the male? This dream was not about sexuality or about gender confusion. It was a comment on an attitude born of feeling disadvantaged as a girl. Can there ever be reconciliation between restraint and repression, shame and expression? Does sexuality only have to be about being 'good' or 'bad'? Does our categorization not need constant redefining and reparation?

It all becomes topsy-turvy. At one level, Freud is right

that every object in a dream is sexual. This is supported by laboratory research that penile tumescence in males, and vaginal wetting in females, accompanies the REM state. Had he lived to know it, the connection would have gladdened Freud's heart. And yet, it has been asked: If everything in a dream is about sex, then what does the sexual act in a dream signify? We saw in Rosie's dream that overtly sexual content may not be about physical sex, but about a totally different issue—in this case, her gender.

Are we then to conclude that dreams signify the opposite of what we dream? Are we back to the ancient belief that if you dream of something good then it portends an upcoming difficulty, and vice versa? The modern axiom is that a dream which is not overtly sexual alludes to its opposite—that is to sexual content—as in the bicycle dream; and when it is blatantly sexual then it may not be alluding directly to sex, like in Rosie's dream. It seems we have entered a fluid zone here without any hard and fast rules about dreams.

~

Let us consider another dream—'Radhika's'.

Her parents were divorced when she was five; she was raised by her mother and grandmother and her relationship with her dad has been tumultuous. Now she is twenty-eight years old. As she said, 'In the last two years, my life has changed immensely. I got married and am going to have a baby. In reality, life is beautiful, really. But since I changed my surroundings, these nightmares have become a recurring phenomenon.'

> *The entire room and situation was dimly lit, grungy. There were unknown people who looked like goons. Typical Hindi movie villains. And then, they wanted to hurt me. Rape, kill or torture. I'm not sure. But definitely something sexual. And instead of fighting back, my reaction or my defence was to comply. And indulge in sexual favours. And be part of the gang. This dream is a recurring one.*

By way of explanation she added after the dream: 'I had been sexually abused as a six-year-old. And my reaction had been to shut down my body and comply.'

Radhika's dream does not fit any of our above categories. It does not signify the opposite of what is portrayed. It is sexually explicit and it is about sexuality, her present and her past. Perhaps the dream is not merely alerting her to something that did happen in the past. Something more is being suggested. Is that why the repetition?

Could it be suggesting a revisiting of the past to allow her to heal?

Moved by her spontaneous disclosure and her courage, I wrote back: 'I hope I can repay your honesty with sensitivity and understanding. Your increasingly active dream life, after your marriage, may be bringing the issue to the fore, suggesting you are now probably strong enough to face and deal with it. As Thomas Hardy staunchly said, "If a way to the Better there be, it exacts a full look at the Worst."'

I specifically asked her, 'Did the abuse happen after your father had left? You must have felt there was no one to protect you. The anger against your father must have surged.'

In reply she sent me another dream.

I am in the house where my father lives. A lady who looks like me but is my mom is sitting there on the bed, next to me. My father walks in and tries to hug a four- or five-year-old girl—that seems to be me. I was pushing him away—saying nasty things and just generally telling him to get away from me. I don't like being held by him.

After that, someone attacked him—either verbally or physically, I'm not sure. I sprung to his defence. Twice.

Radhika said, 'In reality, it is true that I don't like being hugged by him and don't like being his daughter. I hate it actually. But then, when I was staying with him for a short holiday, he had an attack—a coughing fit—and fell straight on the floor, unconscious. I pressed his chest and then he was okay. In that moment, I thought I had lost him and began crying. I don't know why—maybe because of the seriousness of the situation or because I thought I was losing him. I don't really know.'

She continued: 'So, was the dream a third person perspective or was it from the eyes of a four-year-old? I'm not sure. But I feel I deserved more from him. On an intellectual level, I do know I have to forgive him, let go of my anger. But it is still there. I can feel it. And possibly in an attempt to get away from him I might become a bit like him, or so is my fear.

'This was one dream. And dreams around my dad occur frequently.'

I wrote back: 'Did the divorce happen when you were four or five years of age? I ask because in your dream your mom is sitting there on the bed, next to you and your father walks in and tries to hug a girl who is possibly you.'

Even though Radhika hated her father for what he did to her mother and herself, when someone attacked him verbally or physically, she sprung to his defence. And when she feared she was losing him, she was distraught. Was she aware that each of us carries very ambivalent feelings towards the significant people in our lives? We hate and love them. Perhaps love and hate are closely intertwined, mirror images of one another. Even beneath the most loving, caring involvement, hateful and destructive feelings exist. This behaviour is not necessarily pathological but a part of human nature.

The recurrent dreams were a plea from the unconscious—the seemingly irresolvable conflict was that she did not only hate him, but loved him equally. Or else his exit would not have hurt so much. She felt if she admitted any feeling of affection, it could mean exposing herself to hurt again. So she stifled that part, but at a cost. And it sought revenge through recurrent, ambivalent dreams. She hated her father and yet another part of her simultaneously wanted his love. She was repelled by his hugs and at the same time that four- or five-year-old so desperately wanted to be hugged by him.

Radhika wrote back: 'I think there might be a possibility that I blocked out a big chunk of my affection or any positive feelings for my dad while growing up. There is a letter that I have that corroborates this theory—but I dismissed it very early on. I guess you are right—I will have to acknowledge these feelings on a deeper level. How? I still need to figure that one out.

'I had another dream, a very difficult one. It happened a few months ago. And it left quite a vivid picture...

> *Again, I was with someone who seemed to be a sexual deviant and a grown-up version of me. I seemed to be his accomplice. In this case, there was a younger girl who I suspect is me. The girl was around six. And this time I was hurting, abusing her.*

'And the image freaked me out—even in my dream—and when I got up, I remember that emotion very strongly. I never understood what it meant.'

I wrote back to her: 'That six-year-old child is you—when you were that age. And you have been unkind to that child, because you did not know what to do with its pain. So you "abused and hurt her" because you had felt abused and hurt. The sexual deviant part indicates that in a way you perpetuated the violence you perceived had been done to you. You were an accomplice to the shutting down of emotions. You locked up your heart and your body and threw away the key, instinctively, unwittingly. I stepped into your arena of pain by asking you questions about the timing of the divorce and if it happened around six years of age. Or was it when you were four or five years old: the child in the dream who does not like to be hugged? I can only weep for that six-year-old.

'You skirted most of my questions, probably found it difficult to both revisit the reason why your father left and the circumstances of your sexual molestation. Did it happen after your father had left? Are these dreams recreating the event or do they skirt it? I know how difficult these questions are to answer, and it will be totally understandable if you are hesitant too. But if you want to release the pus, you need to incise the boil.

'Sometimes the only way to heal a trauma is to re-enter it in full awareness. What happened in unawareness can only be put right in awareness. Perhaps you may need to accept that you are the best person to look after that child. It can only be nurtured and healed by you. Revisit the site of the incident and help the child negotiate it afresh. Try and be the adult watching the scene. Feel the child's fear and pain. Maybe you could never cry for her. Cry for her now, hold nothing back. Hold that child's trembling body and let it rest against yours as you talk to it, soothe it, and feel true compassion for it. Watch its sobs and trembling settle. Don't leave its side. Look at it with love, with as much love as for the child in your womb. And the child to come will be the beneficiary.'

Radhika wrote back: 'I did go to the house to revisit. Last year. To see it, to feel some sort of emotion. At night I did. It's difficult to feel those things again and move on from there. I can try, I guess.'

In laying bare the dark shapes buried deep in her psyche, dreams helped Radhika set out on the journey to try and come to terms with her past.

Dreams cannot be reduced to a linear, single-purpose phenomenon. They can help explore transgressions, infidelity, incest, alternative or uninhibited sexuality, as also the many other areas and dimensions to love that waking life often does not permit us to explore. I believe dreams about love and sexuality are the most difficult to fully understand. Many questions get raised in the process. What is the distinction between love and sexuality? Can there be love without sexuality? And is sexuality inextricably linked to physicality? When sexuality fades, does love die? And why is literature so full of an unattainable love that never dies?

Perhaps dreams can change our way of looking at love and sexuality separately and together. As historian and social philosopher Eugen Rosenstock-Huessy says: 'Sexuality throws no light upon love, but only through love can we learn to understand sexuality.' Through our dreams, we may become conscious of who we really love, as also of attractions that are as difficult to break as they are to satisfy, as Siddharth discovered...

~

'Siddharth Chauhan' is twenty-seven years old, a postgraduate from an American university now working there. His thumbnail showed a man with a beard that accentuated a fine long face with very gentle eyes. He dreamt:

> *Lita owns a truck that sells something. She sits at the window of the truck and customers come and go. One day, Patsy and Ameeta are visiting this hilly town where Lita and I live. Ameeta goes to the truck to buy something but somehow, she trips and falls and her leg gets stuck in one of the stands supporting the truck. Patsy, I and some others rush to try to save Ameeta who is screaming with pain and in our efforts to save her leg, we have to call a carpenter who has to essentially destroy Lita's truck to free Ameeta's leg.*

> *Over the next few days, I get worried that Lita would like to exact revenge and so I try to walk by her house every now and then to gauge her intentions. I notice that she's turned quieter than before and I can tell this is the silence before a storm. So, I go home and request my mom to let Patsy and Ameeta stay their last two days in our house so they could be protected from any of Lita's bad intentions, but my mom resists. Eventually, I call Patsy and instead my dad picks up (my dad is a doctor). My heart immediately skips a beat (since my dad never knew who Patsy was or that Patsy and I dated for two years), and he says I must come to the hospital since Lita had goons beat both Patsy and Ameeta up. At this point I woke up…*

Siddharth had provided some background to the characters in his dream: '"Patsy" is my ex-girlfriend who I haven't spoken with in four months (I had to let her go, but we still love each other). "Ameeta" is Patsy's best friend. "Lita" is a young girl I met a few weeks ago but it didn't work out with her.'

Dreaming about your ex may point to the need to heal unresolved issues, perhaps the reason for the breakup. But to complicate matters there are two ex-lovers in the dream and they don't seem to be well disposed towards each other. How to unravel this dream with this sparse information? I went back to first principles. Each character in the dream represents some aspect of the dreamer.

I wrote to him: 'The dream seems to be suggesting that your relationship with Lita was a transaction, based on mutual needs, rather than love. Or, at any rate, that was how you perceived it: Lita owns a truck, sells something and has customers. We next come to Ameeta, a close friend of Patsy. Dreams often treat a "close" relationship as a symbol of the person herself. So, is she actually Patsy? Ameeta catches her foot in the stand of the truck and is screaming in pain. Does the pain of your breakup with Patsy still haunt you? Are you feeling "stuck" with the pain? Attempts to save Ameeta don't work, meaning your attempts to heal the wound have not really worked. May we conjecture that you tried to save the relationship with Patsy, but something got further hurt (or destroyed)? To save Ameeta the carpenter has to destroy the truck. Perhaps to save the relationship something else within you needed to be completely changed (or destroyed). You tried to use your relationship with Lita to heal the wound, but since it was a substitute relationship, and Patsy very much still lived in your heart, it could not work out with Lita.

'Perhaps the second part of the dream elucidates the situation. You are trying to gauge Lita's intentions. A storm is brewing in your heart, and in some sense, you want to hit back at Patsy for you are still hurting. The fact that Patsy is still precious to you is symbolized in the dream by your wanting her to stay in your house. Did you feel you did not really know who Patsy was till the breakup?

'You are feeling all "beaten up" inside about both Patsy and Ameeta (the goons beating them up). You need to go to the hospital to heal. Maybe there is something hidden from you (just like your parents don't know about Patsy), something you are unwilling to acknowledge or accept about your relationship with Patsy. This could probably be your contribution to the breakup which needs to be diagnosed and healed (reference to the hospital). Somewhere deep down you are feeling betrayed. But did you also contribute to the betrayal? That question when answered may help with the healing.'

I ended my email by saying: 'I hope this is not too strong a dose. If so, please make allowances for my ignorance of many of the facts of the relationship.'

Siddharth wrote back: 'Five minutes into reading your email, I was tearing up. I don't understand how you got at all this. Everything you have said here is remarkable. These are things that I am too biased to realize myself and perhaps I am too close to the situation to be courageous enough to accept and consciously think about.'

I was struck by the tenacity of love. Siddharth tried to forget Patsy, but the 'forgotten' woman became the template by which he viewed his current relationships. Freud wrote, 'Human beings are funny. They long to be with the person they love but refuse to admit it openly. Some are afraid to show even the slightest sign of affection because of fear. Fear that their feelings may not be recognized or even worst, not returned. But one thing about human beings that puzzles me most is their conscious effort to be connected with the object of their affections even if it kills them slowly within.'

Psychoanalyst Sudhir Kakar says, 'Perhaps it is in the nature of love that one can only truthfully describe the scars it leaves behind, but only incompletely capture what caused the wounds.' Thankfully, there is always a dream that may capture the cause and the wound.

Dreams show the state of our affections as they really

are: not as we conjecture them to be, or as we would like them to be.

~

Next, let us look at a dream of a much older person who also felt the presence of love.

> *Mohan and I have had a baby. The baby has come out awkwardly. When I put it down on the table, it is with a thump. I realize that its head is totally severed from its body. The umbilical cord is coming out of the back of the head and is also lying severed in a twisted coil on the table. I am horrified and repelled.*

'What does such a child mean to you?' I asked.

'Our marriage,' 'Sandhya' said flatly. Her skin still had a porcelain quality to it despite her seventy years. 'Too much disappointment,' she added.

'I am sorry.' She waved aside my attempts at commiseration. She harboured no illusions about a rosy life.

'"Mohan", my husband, first had cancer and is now suffering from an auto-immune disorder. He has become childlike and totally dependent. Since his hearing is failing, he asks me to repeat things louder. I end up shouting. He says I am not adjusting my decibel level. Then when I try and modulate my voice to adjust to his hearing he says I am deliberately talking softly so that he cannot catch what I am saying. He then becomes petulant and shoves me away, saying I am not in tune with his needs. I feel rejected, he feels rejected, and we end up squabbling over inessentials.'

'And what do you think the child's severed head represents?'

'After this dream I felt a great pain that lasted for a week.' Her large eyes were expressive as she rested her hand on her heart.

I wondered if it was a pain from the past which had seeped into her dream, short-circuited itself to hinge onto other issues. How does one sort out and restore emotions to where they belong? In the dream, the child born from the marriage lies with its head severed. The head seems further emphasized by the severed umbilical cord attached to it.

'Was the marriage always a "head" thing, a practical arrangement where your heart was never involved?'

'Isn't that how it usually is?'

Silence was an easy way out. Ambivalence, as said earlier, is part of all intimate relationships. But Sandhya was suggesting her heart was never involved even though it was a 'love' marriage. That was strange: why?

'After a week of pain, could you figure out why?'

'Something about marriage itself…or maybe something even before that,' her voice was low. Memory seemed to have spun a cocoon around her.

'I was married once before. It was a painful, violent marriage. Once he beat me up so much that I was hospitalized. I appealed to my father, but he felt I should go back. I stayed with my brother for a while, and then, frightened and bruised, I limped back to my husband. Ultimately, I had to find the way out of the marriage on my own.'

Perhaps, after this traumatic experience, she had

emotionally shut down. And when the current marriage had its unsettling moments, it reminded her of the far worse past, whose pain had been submerged but never forgotten. The dream had emphasized the head twice. A reference to the two marriages? The wound of her grief was fully exposed. Could it now be debrided, the scarred tissue removed, so as to allow it to heal straight and true?

'Who or what are you grieving for now?'

To my surprise she didn't choose any of the options I had set before her. 'I think I am grieving for love.'

'Do you feel you were denied love or you denied it to yourself?'

'I did not make myself available for love. I had decided earlier—no involvement, no pain.' The beheaded, grotesque baby that could have lived with love, but died mangled in pain.

'Do you believe that being loved is a matter of sheer chance? Or can we influence it?'

'I have been influenced by it.'

The statement had a ring of authenticity to it. I grew curious. 'How?'

She hesitated as though unsure how to put words to the inexpressible, then said, 'I was at the height of my suffering with my first husband. He was a drunk, abusive and physically violent. One day I was at some family puja, sitting cross-legged on the ground. I was a mass of sorrow. Then suddenly it happened. Out of the blue. I don't know how or why, but it was unforgettable.'

The moment seemed to demand the pause of silence between us.

'This incredible feeling of sweetness slowly rose up

from my feet and flooded every recess of my body. I don't know how to describe it. It was like the nectar of love, bliss. I was soaked in it. There was no person there to love or be loved by. Just the flood gates opened, every pore of mine was drenched in love itself.'

By osmosis, I too felt its power. The silence was longer this time.

'This experience wiped clean the bitterness I had for my first husband. I could view him quite objectively. After this, I did not feel sorry for myself.'

There seemed a deeper mystery at work here. The love Sandhya was soaked in was not for someone or felt by someone for her. It was just love—unattached, undiluted, unentangled with expectations from people or things. A state of being that reflected a deeper harmony.

What is this boundless state, this great domain of love which can enter the small house of our lives, reminding us of the cadence of an old song, of a joy once known?

As Rabindranath Tagore said, 'Love is an endless mystery, for it has nothing else to explain it.'

Yet it raises the question that if Sandhya had been imbued with the power of love, why the dream of a severed baby's head and the twisted coils lying on the table? Had the experience of love not modified or transformed her perceptions? Maybe to fully absorb the import of such an experience one has to unravel, unwind consciously all the fears and scars, keeping that moment of illumination as the yardstick to measure all that still remains unresolved in the psyche. There may have been an epiphany but how does one allow one's personality to feel its infusion constantly? Was Sandhya's dream a reminder to her of all the areas she still needed to restore in the light of that experience?

For love as we know it through its many faces is tangled by human passions and its fallibilities, existing in an exhaustingly untidy world.

But still it is love, with its ability to dissolve everything, making the broken whole, the only glue to the separate pieces of our aloneness, a music whose source none knows.

Ashishda had once said, 'Love, or Eros, is the power which has brought the whole universe into being and holds it together as a unity. Through its manifestations in the world of multiplicity, [Love] seeks to find and to know the absolute unity of its essential nature.'

Was Sandhya confirming that love had come spontaneously, a power or a force that poured its melody over the rocky bed of her sorrow, wearing it down, in fact dissolving it?

8. Not One Drop of My Self-Worth Depends on Your Acceptance of Me

'Doel' awoke feeling very disturbed. She had dreamt about 'Mrinalini'—once her closest friend—for the first time. Lying in bed, she tried to recollect the dream. It slowly came back to her. But why was it bothering her so much? So much so that later that day her body was burning with fever.

> *Mrinalini appeared. I was aware that she was no more. I asked her about it. She told me something, which I couldn't recall.*

Two months earlier, barely out of school, Mrinalini had committed suicide. This fact alone made Doel believe that the dream was about Mrinalini—that she was helping Doel make peace with the shock of her death. If dreams are essentially a commentary on the dreamer's personal life and attitudes, can they, so to speak, step out of line and objectively comment on someone else whom they loved? The dream could not be about Mrinalini alone. In some essential way it had to be a reflection both of Doel herself and of her relationship with Mrinalini prior to the suicide.

Over the next few months, the dream repeated itself following the same pattern:

> *Mrinalini appears. She tells me something, which I could never recall. She dies again, each time in a different way—hanging, drowning, poisoning.*
>
> *I wake up feeling ill.*

With every repetition, what was the dream drawing Doel's attention to? Repetitive dreams, we know, remind the dreamer about something that has not been come to terms with. What had Doel missed about herself in her assumption that the repetitive dream was only about Mrinalini? Doel still couldn't see how her dream had anything to do with her and instead focused on the trajectory of their relationship to grasp what had compelled Mrinalini to end her life tragically.

They had known each other since they were kids. More than Mrinalini herself, it was her parents who obsessed about Mrinalini emerging as the topper in everything—academics, elocution, singing. The year Doel had come first in class, Mrinalini's parents spread the canard that her father had a secret understanding with the teachers which had led to her scoring well in the exams. Mrinalini too repeated the story. Finding this difficult to handle, Doel distanced herself from Mrinalini and the two went from being close friends to mere classmates. And all this had happened when they were in Class 4!

Over the years, Mrinalini had become a loner, feeling jealous of any classmates who performed better than her. Her isolation was compounded by her parents having fought with almost every other parent. However, Doel could never forget the strange reversal in their relationship that occurred when they were in Class 12.

She was upset and sitting alone in the classroom when Mrinalini came up, sat beside her and asked her why she was upset. Doel spontaneously shared her feelings. Consolingly, Mrinalini assured her that soon things would be just fine. The intervening years melted away as they talked for a while longer. Doel returned home feeling regretful that they weren't as close as before. Four months later, on June 21, 2008, at about 11.00 am, Mrinalini had committed suicide by hanging herself!

Stranger still, at 3.30 am that same morning, Doel had woken up breathless and afraid. She woke up her mother and told her she didn't know why she was so terrified. She couldn't go back to sleep and switched on the lights, waiting for dawn to break.

June 21 was also Doel's mother's birthday. That year, her father was out of town. She was in the middle of lunch at a restaurant with her sister and mother when her father called to give them the news. Her mother immediately rushed to Mrinalini's house. Doel wept inconsolably. Some of her friends went to say their final goodbyes. But Doel could not bring herself to see Mrinalini one last time. She felt she would never recover from the sight of seeing her dead. In the days to come, she kept imagining her body hanging from the ceiling and wishing that Mrinalini's parents had saved her. Two months later the dreams followed.

At one level, the dream is about Mrinalini and her low self-worth which culminated in the forcible and violent ending of her life. Yet, there must have been something within Doel that was so wrought up that it blocked her from saying a final goodbye. It seems her hurt had put a lid on her feelings for Mrinalini, maybe completely eclipsing them. Could that be why dreams of Mrinalini came to her repeatedly? To make Doel accept her buried feelings for Mrinalini? Instead, Doel kept wishing for things to have turned out differently: If only Mrinalini's parents could have prevented it! Could this be an inversion of her own guilt of not renewing her friendship with Mrinalini sooner, which possibly could have prevented her suicide?

Perhaps the dream was as much about Doel's mixed-up feelings and her scarred relationship with Mrinalini. It was not merely a bereavement dream where the dead person appears and her death is relived. Supporting this belief were three other dreams that came to Doel.

Mrinalini was in prison with other children. She wasn't eighteen years old in my dreams but about twelve or thirteen. She walked out of a prison cell and asked me whether I could get her some 50-50 biscuits. (I don't remember her liking those biscuits. Neither was I a huge fan of them.) I went out to buy the biscuits. There I met a few other friends. I told them excitedly that Mrinalini wasn't dead and that I had seen her. They wouldn't believe me. So I took them along to see for themselves. But then, Mrinalini disappeared. Leaving behind the others, I walked a little further, down a dark alley with prison cells on either side. At the end of it, I found her and gave her the biscuits. She thanked me and told me she didn't want to meet other people.

Prisons often represent the traps we create for ourselves. It may seem that external circumstances imprison us making life difficult, but in actual fact we may be the creators of those circumstances. Mrinalini's desire to be numero uno in everything, which was obsessively fuelled by her parents, became an unbearable burden for her to carry. Her prison. Her inability to fulfil this desire would have eroded Mrinalini's self-worth, eventually leading to the suicide. But is Mrinalini the only one in prison? In the dream there are also other children in this prison, as is Doel—walking down a dark alley with prison cells on either side. Could this not clearly signify that those other children, including Doel, were also imprisoned by the belief of topping their class? A not-too-uncommon belief among many students. Also, Doel's not going to Mrinalini's house, unlike the other school friends, is possibly indicative of a conflict deep within her. If competitiveness had plagued Mrinalini and contributed to her low self-worth, had Doel herself not been equally stricken by it? Other elements in the dream also lend to this conjecture.

Mrinalini walks out of the prison cell. Perhaps death was the only option she had to free herself of the oppression of worthlessness! The dream is asking: How can Doel negotiate her sense of guilt?

Then Mrinalini asks for some 50-50 biscuits. What does this metaphor indicate? We can try to explore the multiple meanings it could give rise to. Could it be about both of them (50:50) viewing things through the distorted lens of low self-esteem? Again, on the one hand, the metaphor could signify the unwitting choice that had tilted the balance (50:50) for Mrinalini that fateful morning; on the other hand, it could be indicating that

Doel, similarly driven by issues of self-esteem, played an equal part (50:50) in their ruptured relationship. This would suggest Doel suffered equally from a fear of failure as Mrinalini, that she was similarly imprisoned. So that each mirrored the other, and in disowning the other they ended up disowning what belonged to them.

The allusion to the age of 12–13 could be about Class 12—Mrinalini had befriended a solitary and upset Doel, even though they were no longer friends. Telling the friends in the dream that Mrinalini was not dead could be expressing Doel's desire to reverse the clock so she could have had one more chance to act differently. Possibly, deep down she was regretful for letting her feelings of affront dictate her perceptions of Mrinalini. And more importantly, that regret had frozen her and not allowed her to even say a final goodbye.

In the dream, the friends don't believe Doel that Mrinalini is not dead. Nor does Mrinalini want to meet them. This may suggest that this is a private matter between Mrinalini and Doel and not in the public domain. The juxtaposition of friends believing Mrinalini is dead and Doel telling them she is alive highlights that something believed to be dead is actually alive. Is the dream suggesting that Doel has to engage with this 'dead' issue—her psychic deadness to Mrinalini? That it is time to accept and acknowledge this? Only then can she give her the 50-50 biscuits. Biscuits that neither of them particularly cared for (accepted) but that needed to be purchased (acknowledged) in order for both to understand what had driven them apart.

As Maxwell Maltz says: 'Low self-esteem is like driving

through life with your hand-brake on.' And dreams can start a dialogue, helping us locate why and when the hand brakes came on. Or can it be a fifty-fifty situation, where the dreamer and the one being dreamt of are both commented on by the dream?

Doel's next dream was interesting.

> *Mrinalini appeared in a white dress. By this time, I had started getting conscious in my dreams. I was feeling a little afraid on seeing her. She told me she was my friend and that there was nothing to fear. Next, she took my hand and we were flying in the sky.*

The ability to fly is possibly indicative that Doel had broken the prison wall that had bound them both. Perhaps she had accepted her part in their relationship. Paradoxically, her doing so released them.

Then Doel had one final dream after which she never dreamt of Mrinalini again.

> *I was attending a marriage ceremony. But somehow I didn't know whose marriage it was. Then suddenly, I found myself in a room where the bride was getting decked up. I walked up to her. And then Mrinalini turned towards me, asking me how she looked. I told her that she looked beautiful.*

A marriage is a union, an integration of two opposite pulls in the dreamer. No longer did Doel only see the rupture in their relationship, or Mrinalini's traumatic end belonging only to Mrinalini. By accepting the fact that she contributed to it, she is able to see the beauty in Mrinalini and in their relationship. She no longer needed to dream of her again, because a healing had taken place at a deeper level.

~

Wanting to be someone else seems like a waste of what a person really is. The question that arises is: Why do we so easily mortgage our identity to the claims of others?

Are 'Sakshi's' dreams another example of this? In fact, she had three dreams—a series—that are thematically related. Thirty years old, originally from Delhi, she did two years of grad school and took up a job as the development director of a software company in the US. She had lived with her mother. She had not seen her father since she was about two or three and this had impacted her strongly. She said, 'Of late I have been facing some physical injuries (specifically on my right foot for a few months) and dealing with some body image issues that I have not been able to figure out for several years. I have been living happily by myself in California. I love my job and my team, my boss is great and he appreciates my work. There is just one problem—I find it difficult to work with a junior colleague, "Mike", who is a loud white man and is the same age as me.'

Let's start with her last dream dated June 14 first and see how the story unfolds from there.

> *My entire work team goes on a drive in India (though we actually work in the US). I call my two friends in Bangalore and ask them to join my team outing. They come. We are taking a group photo—I happen to be the shortest because everyone else is standing on a stool. Part of this dream was embarrassing. I was*

> in a toilet for an hour in the dream. Clothes get dirty and they need to be washed. My mom is checking on me. Part of the dream I am worried and holding my niece closely. I am looking at her and her eyes become green (which they are not in real). Her mom, who is my cousin sister, is there and I am telling her '...your daughter is so cute', and I am holding on to my niece tight.

Usually the most bizarre part of the dream is the most telling: 'We are taking a group photo—I happen to be the shortest because everyone else is standing on a stool.'

Does Sakshi feel disadvantaged because everyone else in the group is of a good height, while she is the 'shortest'. Here height is a metaphor for stature (qualifications, looks, money, family prestige, fame, established identity). A group photograph could be a snapshot of an objective portrayal of how she sees herself—short or falling 'short' in comparison to her friends and colleagues who she views as more entitled than her.

Her clothes get soiled in the toilet and need to be washed. This 'shitty' soiled self-image she holds of herself needs to be evacuated. She is afraid that if she faces this image, it would make her feel worse instead of feeling better. But the dream informs her otherwise. It tells her to change the way of thinking of herself as 'soiled'; not only will it bring new life (green is the colour of growth, renewal, Nature—the green eyes of her young niece), it will give her new 'eyes' to view herself. If only she would take off the spectacles of low self-esteem, she would find herself immensely lovable, huggable like her niece. The

My Self-Worth Doesn't Depend on Your Acceptance | 145

worst self-punishment one can inflict is of banishing oneself as being unacceptable.

June 13:

I was climbing many trees. I kept going further without knowing and suddenly I turn back to see how far I have come. In the third or fourth tree, something pokes my leg—like a thorn. I try to pull it out—it becomes a worm and I fling it off. I remember feeling frightened when the thorn turns into a worm.

Did this internal sense of 'shittiness' start when she was around three or four years old (reference to the 'third or fourth tree')? 'Something pokes my leg—like a thorn.' What were the 'thorny' circumstances, sexual or otherwise that led her to feeling used, belittled, denigrated, inferior (like a worm)? Yet she has climbed high enough in the tree of age and maturity to view the 'thorn [that] turn[ed] into a worm'.

June 11:

My entire office was sitting in a classroom. My boss Harry turns to Mike, my junior, and says, 'Like, are you sure you want to take over this with the kind of person you are?' Jake thinks it's about his body. He feels like he is on the fatter side. Ben says, 'I am not talking about your body but I am talking about your attitude.' Then goes on to say, 'Your attitude has been a problem. If you take on this bigger project, I don't think your attitude will be satisfactory.' I agree. In the next scene, I am going to wash my face in something that looks like a washbasin in an ISKCON temple and people are asking for money.

The water is not very clear. I meet two girls but I don't remember who they are.

The entire office is in a classroom. 'Classroom' here is a metaphor for a learning opportunity.

Sakshi's attitude towards herself and her body seems to be the problem. She worries she is on the 'fatter side'. The dream suggests that is not the real problem—it is 'about your attitude', the view she has of herself that she is really no good, unworthy. The dream is asking: Is this the kind of attitude you need towards yourself?

If she is to take on a 'bigger project', that is move towards greater self-assurance, then her current attitude is inadequate for that 'project'. Sakshi understands that she needs to 'wash her face', or cleanse herself of this fixation of having a faulty body and face. This attitude 'muddies' her emotions (water represents feelings). It makes her unsure of who she is (she meets two girls and can't remember who they are).

It's interesting how dreams peg significant years in our childhood where either the trauma is located or where the dreamer's self-representation began to take shape. For Sakshi it was at the age of three or four. A number in a dream may indicate a personal meaning, such as a significant anniversary, the death of a loved one, or the number of a house we once lived in. We may not consciously remember it but our mind often retains the significance of such numbers. But can an object, like a cupboard, lock up not only memories but one's self-worth as well? I have broken the next dream into sections to elucidate this.

~

'Aakriti' dreamt:

> I enter a classroom. I am not sitting with the other students, but right next to the door, facing the students rather than the teacher. My seat is at the very edge of the room, almost as though I am not really part of it. In front of me is a dark brown wall cupboard.

The dream continues:

> The class begins, and shortly after, the teacher (he's someone new, who hasn't taught the class before) and his assistant are asked by some authorities to come out of the class. For some reason, I now find myself outside the classroom, with the teacher and his aide. We are being questioned about something, some shady activity they're involved in, a theft of some sort.

The dream is trying to locate a memory that goes back to school or a classroom where a 'shady' incident took place. Shady in the sense that it was not a black and white issue and may have been open to interpretation—an incident perhaps in which Aakriti had been implicated (she is part of the threesome). She had been doubted, 'questioned', and in the process may have been robbed of something essential—acceptability. At first, she is hardly part of the class, and then the interrogation 'takes her out of the class', a metaphor for feeling left out in the cold.

The dream story continues:

> Then, I'm back to the classroom, sitting at the same spot in front of the cupboard. I am stressed out because I realize that this cupboard contains all my

stuff and I need to pack it up. There's so much stuff in that cupboard that it's making me feel anxious. I don't know how or where to pack all of it.

Is the cupboard somehow linked to the 'shady' incident? Most of the drama of the dream is centred on this cupboard. Acknowledging its significance, Aakriti is sitting in front of it. Much 'stuff' or painful memories are locked in there. How will she 'pack' or rather unpack it all? She is anxious. A cupboard may symbolize things we wish to keep hidden. Things in our psyche that are 'locked away'.

Back to the dream.

I'm sorting through the cupboard; some student comes up to me, looking at me somewhat accusingly—as if to ask why I am sorting through the classroom supplies cupboard. The lines are blurred, as they tend to be in the dream, on what this cupboard is or what it is supposed to contain.

Earlier she was interrogated outside the classroom for theft, and on opening the cupboard she was accused of stealing. She is unsure what this cupboard actually contains. Though she is brave enough to open the cupboard in an attempt to face what is in it, something in there prevents her from a full disclosure of its contents. This dream illustrates how we may reach the site of trauma and yet be unable to zoom in on the memory of the problem's inception.

In the dream she says:

I try to explain to that student, a girl, that all of this is my stuff, and that I'm actually an adult whose soul has somehow come into a schoolgirl's body. That I have lived many years and then suddenly for some reason I'm back at school and look like a teenager. She doesn't seem convinced, so I show her some photos of me in college and in my later years. The photos are of someone who looks like a grown-up version of me so she believes me.

In search of the genesis of the issue, she tries to go back into a 'schoolgirl's body' or revisit the past, through her school, teenage and college years. Photos are memory snapshots. So she is trying to tell herself that she has 'grown up', and manages to convince herself and the student of it. All the same the feeling that the contents of the cupboard will explain more about her true identity persists in her. Those photographs in the cupboard were essential to reveal her state of being to her.

Aakriti is a thirty-one-year-old journalist. In the recent past this classroom has appeared in her dreams three or four times. Actually, she had studied in four different schools. She said, 'In my recent dreams, the school or the students that are usually in class are my friends from the school where I spent the longest time, five years, from Class 6 to Class 10.'

Did the part of the dream where the teacher, his assistant and Aakriti find themselves outside the classroom occur when she was between Classes 6 and 10? Aakriti said it happened in Class 7.

That apart, the cupboard had another association for Aakriti. She said, 'Something like this happened to me in reality about two and a half years ago. I took a sabbatical from work in 2016 and moved from Mumbai to Delhi, where my parents lived. I was planning to move back to Mumbai eventually so I hadn't cleared out my stuff from my apartment. My boyfriend was occupying it while I was away and paying my share of the rent. In late 2016, I had decided to permanently move to Delhi for a few years, so I made a trip to Mumbai to take the rest of my stuff from the apartment. A few days into that trip, I learnt that my boyfriend had cheated on me sometime earlier that year. I cut my trip short and booked a ticket back to Delhi. I was really shocked and in no position to sort through and pack my stuff. There were books, furniture, clothes, vessels, etc., so it wasn't a straightforward process. Eventually, I took some of the stuff and my friends and boyfriend cleared out the rest.'

No doubt later the cupboard also represented the pain of her boyfriend's betrayal as she was *'in no position to sort through and pack my stuff'*. A statement that applies both to the physical and the emotional stuff. But the dream cupboard seems to contain more than that. It seems her boyfriend's betrayal had only added another layer over the original betrayal felt in school. What could that be?

Aakriti said, 'I keep struggling with the feeling that I'm not good enough, essentially.'

And does that cupboard still hold on to its secret, when the seeds of feeling 'not good enough' were sowed?

Carl Rogers, an advocate of humanistic psychology, felt the source of many people's problems is that they consider themselves worthless and incapable of being loved.

Much psychological research has been done with the underlying idea that low self-esteem is the root of the problem for many individuals, leading to many societal problems. A leading figure of the movement, psychologist Nathaniel Branden stated, 'I cannot think of a single psychological problem—from anxiety and depression, to fear of intimacy or of success, to spouse battery or child molestation—that is not traced back to the problem of low self-esteem.'

Experiences in a person's life are a major source of how self-esteem develops. Right from our childhood we are influenced and imposed on by the norms of the day, and are constantly adapting to outside pressures. In the early years of a child's life, parents have a significant influence on their self-esteem and may be the main source of shaping it. Unconditional love from parents includes being sensitively listened to and spoken to respectfully, receiving appropriate affection and attention, having accomplishments recognized and mistakes and failures acknowledged and accepted. All of this translates into self-esteem in the child. On the other hand, being harshly criticized, emotionally ridiculed, physically or sexually abused, constantly held in comparison to others or expected to be 'perfect' leads to lack of validation and devaluation in the child. And as has been seen in the dreams of people above, it is far simpler to build up the child than restore the adult.

~

If the damage has taken place, how can it be repaired later in life? The dream below is of a woman in her fifties, who was adopted from an orphanage at the age of five. Her adoptive father died soon after her arrival in her new home, leaving her adoptive mother totally distraught. 'Alka' grew up to be a psychologist, is married and has two children. But the child she once was knocked at her door, asking to be spoken to.

> There is a mall where a five-year-old child is going from shop to shop looking for someone. I am standing and watching this child's distress. Suddenly, a lift comes in the centre where I am standing. I get in and as the lift rises, I continue to watch the child with a pang of sadness. I feel the higher I go up (in age and distance) I will lose touch with that child, never being able to reconnect with her again. But then as the lift reaches the halfway point, the sadness goes as the child turns around and I smile at her. The moment of contact felt so real, because the child recognizes me and yet we have never met.

This dream has everything. There's the number five, the age at which she was adopted, and when it may have made her wonder who her parents really were. She is going from shop to shop, that is, she is searching for her sense of belonging. And this time the lift opens to reveal its contents. It reveals the child she once was, rarely sighted in the growing years towards maturity, but whose presence is felt in patterns of behaviour, in fears and anxieties, and in the panic of not knowing where home is. Alka watches the child first at ground level, then, as the lift rises, from the distance of an adult view. The beauty of the dream is that the child and the adult make a real contact, recognize one another, and perhaps with that a shift occurs from the gaze of the wounded child to that of the adult. Perhaps it is time for Alka to say to that child, 'You are me, and yet not. I am truly sorry for your pain, which you once had to handle all by yourself. But today, I know of it, feel it and look at you with all the compassion you deserve. You are not lost (orphaned), as I am your true mother. I will look after you, hear you, and comfort you as once I could not.' In the process, maybe both the mother and child came home.

9. The Snake Catches Its Tail: Breakthrough Dreams

If I were to say to you that the diabetic insulin shot that saved lives in your family, or that the beautiful dress you coveted in the shop window, or that the GPS which takes you to your destination safely were the direct or indirect results of dreams, would you believe it? Probably not. No twist in the tail here. It so happens that they are. In fact a whole industry owes its livelihood to Elias Howe's invention of the sewing machine, which was heralded by dream imagery. People had been trying to fabricate such a device for half a century in America and elsewhere without much success. Howe spent five years trying to develop a model of the sewing machine and repeatedly failed, because he always made the needle with the thread-hole in the middle of the shank. Then one night he dreamt:

He has been captured by a tribe of savages, who take him to their king.

'Elias Howe,' roared the monarch, 'I command you on pain of death to finish this machine at once.'

Cold sweat poured down his brow as he saw himself surrounded by dark-skinned warriors, whose faces and chests are painted and who formed a hollow square about him as they lead him to the place of execution. Suddenly he noticed that near the heads of the spears which his guards carried, there were eye-shaped holes.

He had solved the riddle! What he needed was a needle with an eye near the point![1]

He had got his breakthrough. He sprang out of bed, and at once made an eye-pointed needle. It worked.

The discovery that brought hope to diabetics came to Sir Frederick Banting in its totality when he awoke from sleep. Thousands of people around the world afflicted with diabetes, especially children, had no hope of survival since all attempts to isolate insulin so far had been unsuccessful. On the night of October 30, 1920, while preparing a lecture on diabetes, Banting fell asleep. At two o'clock in the morning, he woke up and scribbled these sentences: 'Tie up the duct of the pancreas of a dog. Wait for a few weeks until the glands shrivel up. Then cut it out, wash it out and filter the precipitation.'[2]

Banting put to test these sleep instructions in a laboratory. He tied up the pancreatic duct of a dog and waited for seven weeks, and then he cut open the dog to see if the pancreas had shrunk in size. Since it had not, he repeated the experiment till the desired result was attained. He was able to extract insulin from the pancreas and inject it into a diabetic dog that was dying. The dog soon sat up wagging its tail.

On January 11, 1922, Banting injected insulin into a fourteen-year-old boy dying of diabetes at Toronto General Hospital. Almost immediately his blood sugar levels fell;

within days, he was out of bed, and within weeks he was home, though dependent on insulin injections. The world applauded Frederick Banting, and he was awarded the Nobel Prize.

As a young man Albert Einstein had a dream of critical importance to the history of science. 'He dreamt he was speeding down a steep mountainside on a sled. He went faster and faster and as he approached the speed of light he noticed that the stars above him were refracting light into a spectra of colours that he had never seen before. This image impressed him so deeply that he never forgot it, maintaining that his entire scientific achievement had been the result of meditating on that dream. It provided the basis of the "thought experiment" through which he worked out the principle of relativity.'[3]

Besides the enormous impact of Einstein's theory in the pure sciences, his 'thought experiment' impacts our daily lives. Without the proper application of the Theory of Relativity, the Global Positioning System (GPS) would fail in its navigational functions in a couple of minutes affecting military equipment, airplane navigation, oil exploration and, of course, how would you find your way home if lost during a trekking expedition!

Another dream helped shape the course of India's freedom struggle. It was the year 1919 when the draconian Rowlatt Bill—that would give the ruling British government powers to arrest any person on suspicion without a warrant—was likely to be gazetted into an act. Protest against the bill was unequivocal. All pleas to the Viceroy that the bill was not only harsh but also unjust left the British government undeterred. The threat of the bill becoming an act mounted. Freedom from tyranny was the cry of the nation. But how was it to be effected? One man meditated on this problem for weeks. Then he had a dream on the strength of which he initiated a nationwide *satyagraha* movement (a policy of non-violent political resistance) in India. The man was Mohandas Karamchand Gandhi.

Gandhi's great quandary was to figure out how Indians could offer resistance to a bill whose tyrannical powers had still not been brought into operation. Against what were the Indians to offer *satyagraha*? Gandhi had experimented with *satyagraha* during his days in South Africa and also in a few local cases in India, but never at a national scale. How was he to galvanize an entire nation to resist tyranny without succumbing to violence in the process?

While Gandhi was pondering over these questions news came in that the Rowlatt Bill had been passed. That night he fell asleep, deeply perplexed about the issue. In his autobiography he writes: 'The idea came to me last night in a dream that we should call upon the country to observe a general *hartal* [a strike that calls for the closure of all places of business, courts of law and schools, as a mark of protest or sorrow]. Satyagraha is a process of self-purification, and ours is a sacred fight, and it seems to me to be in the fitness of things that it should be commenced with an act of self-purification. Let all the people of India, therefore, suspend their business on that day and observe the day as one of fasting and prayer.'[4]

Gandhi declared April 6 as the day of the *hartal*. The message reached the four corners of the country and the whole of India, every town and village, observed a complete *hartal* on that day.

From an idea born in a dream, a nation demonstrated phenomenal collective will as 'soul' force won over brute force.

Was this one great man's isolated dream or is history replete with examples of people who have heeded their dreams and changed the course of human thought? In every field—from science, sports, literature, art, philosophy and film-making, to the winning and losing of wars—the creative process of dreaming has offered revolutionary insights. Often the dreamer is consciously working on a problem when a dream suddenly provides him or her with a crucial hint.

Neils Bohr, one of the key figures in the genesis of modern atomic physics, had a vivid dream when he was a student. He was standing on the surface of a sun composed of burning gas. Planets whistled past him, each of them attached to the sun by a thin filament. 'Suddenly, the gas sun cooled and solidified, the planets crumbled away.'[5] In 1913 this was the commonly held picture of the atom: a central, positively charged nucleus (the sun) around which orbit negatively charged electrons (the planets). This model, however, left some crucial questions unanswered. If the atom contained a concentrated positive charge at its centre, why were the electrons not drawn into its centre?

While engrossed with this problem Bohr had another powerful dream that led to the formulation of his famous atomic theory. 'He was at the races. The horses ran in lanes, which were clearly marked with white dust. They were permitted to change lanes provided they maintained a distance between one another. If a horse ran along a white line and kicked up dust, however, it was immediately disqualified.'[6]

When he awoke, this 'rule of the track' gave Bohr the clue to the structure of the atom. His theory states that electrons orbit the atomic nucleus in circular (or more generally elliptical) orbits. The electrons can orbit only in certain well-defined orbits, just as horses have to keep to the lanes. As long as the electron remains in a given orbit it emits no energy and continues to circle around the nucleus. They can change orbits only by gaining or losing energy, but they cannot travel in the intermediate space lying in between these well-defined orbits. The horse would be disqualified for running outside its defined lane.

Bohr found this notion 'so exciting that he postponed his honeymoon to write what became a landmark paper'.[7] On the basis of this insight Bohr was awarded a Nobel Prize in 1922. Perhaps quantum theory has much to thank the dreaming mind for than it would care to admit!

Friedrich August Kekule, a professor of chemistry in Ghent, Belgium, had been grappling for years with the critical problem of solving the molecular structure of benzene. Driven to distraction at not finding a solution, one evening in 1865, he fell asleep in his chair next to the fire, and dreamt one of the most significant dreams of scientific history. He relates: 'Again the atoms were gambolling before my eyes. This time the smaller groups kept modestly in the background. My mental eye, rendered more acute by repeated visions of this kind, could now distinguish larger structures, of manifold conformation; long rows, sometimes more closely fitted together; all twining and twisting in snakelike motion. But look! What was that? One of the snakes had seized hold of its own tail, and the form whirled mockingly before my eyes. As if by a flash of lightning I awoke...'[8]

What is now taken for granted in chemistry was unknown then—that the molecular structure of benzene is in the form of a chain of molecules arranged in the shape of a hexagonal ring with an atom of carbon and of hydrogen at each point of the hexagon. The benzene ring, as it is called, presented itself to Kekule in a dream in the form of a snake grabbing hold of its own tail. The revolutionary discovery was hailed as the 'most brilliant piece of prediction to be found in the whole range of organic chemistry'.

It is no surprise therefore that Kekule, relating his dream-discovered insight to a scientific convention in 1890, exhorted his colleagues: 'Let us learn to dream, gentlemen, and then we may perhaps find the truth.'

Echoing Kekule is Larry Page, the co-founder of Google. In 2009, at the commencement address at the University of Michigan, he shared how he first conceived the idea of Google. He dreamt he had somehow managed to download the entire Web and just keep the links. This became the basis for the algorithm to power a new search engine now known as Google. Referring to the above dream that triggered his quest to develop a search engine, Page said, 'You know what it is like to wake up in the middle of the night with a vivid dream? And you know that if you don't have a pencil and paper by the bed, it will be completely gone by the morning. Sometimes it is important to wake up and stop dreaming. When a really great dream shows up, grab it.'

Now herein lies the paradox. Kekule in the field of chemistry, Bohr in the microcosmic world of atoms, and Einstein in the macrocosmic sphere of stars and galaxies were men who were pioneers in modern science—a branch of knowledge whose entire basis is objectivity, logicality and verifiability. However, reversing this scientific credo these men displayed their dependence on mental processes that are intuitive and verifiable only after the event. On reading extracts from their autobiographies and letters without knowing who they are, they would be perceived as a bunch of romantic poets or artists. Several remarkable qualities underscore their work and run through their writings: the setting aside of logic and deductive reasoning except when verifying an insight; a deep aversion for the one-track mind; a distrust of the scientific demands for consistency; and scepticism towards an all-too-conscious thinking. This sceptical reserve is compensated by trust in intuition and unconscious insights.[9]

Dream insights can occur in two ways: they can either provide the solution to a problem in its totality, in clear and literal terms, as was seen in the case of Banting, or they can furnish the symbolic idea from which the solution emerges.

Dream insights also helped Otto Loewi win the Nobel Prize in 1936, in Physiology and Medicine. Loewi, like Banting, noted down an experiment that changed the perception of the functioning of the human body. Once again the solution appeared in his dream in its totality. Prior to Loewi's time it was assumed that nervous impulses in the body were transmitted by an electrical wave. Loewi, during a conversation with a colleague in 1903, conceived the idea that there might be a chemical transmission of the nervous impulse, rather than an electrical one, but he saw no way of proving his hunch and it slipped from his conscious memory, only to emerge again in 1920.

'The night before Easter Sunday of that year [1920] I awoke, turned on the light, and jotted down a few notes on a tiny slip of thin paper. Then I fell asleep again. It occurred to me at six o'clock in the morning that during the night I had written down something most important, but I was unable to decipher the scrawl. The next night, at three o'clock, the idea returned. It was the design of an experiment to determine whether or not the hypothesis of chemical transmission that I had uttered seventeen years ago was correct. I got up immediately, went to the laboratory, and performed a simple experiment on a frog's heart according to the nocturnal design... Its results became the foundation of the theory of chemical transmission of the nervous impulse.'[10]

It appears that creativity, like dreaming, relies heavily on the unconscious. Loewi's idea that there might be a chemical transmission of the nervous impulse gestated for seventeen long years before he saw a way to prove his hunch. The thought slipped from his conscious mind, but it seems that his unconscious kept working on it, as the design of an experiment crystallized in 1920.

French polymath Henri Poincare, who pioneered the chaos theory in mathematics, believed that mathematical talent is essentially dependent on unconscious processes. 'When one is working on a difficult problem,' wrote Poincare, 'it often happens that at the start of the work one makes no progress. One then allows oneself a shorter or longer break for rest and thereafter sits down again at one's desk. During the first half-hour one again finds nothing, and then suddenly the decisive idea presents itself... Probably unconscious work went on during the rest period, and the result of this labour is later revealed...'[11]

Similar experiences seem to be the rule rather than the exception and have been reported by other mathematicians. Jacques Hadamard stated: '...One phenomenon is certain and I can vouch for its absolute certainty: the sudden and immediate appearance of a solution at the very moment of sudden awakening. On being very abruptly awakened by an external noise, a solution long searched for appeared to me at once without the slightest instant of reflection on my part—the fact was remarkable enough to have struck me unforgettably—and in quite different direction from any of those which I had previously tried to follow.'[12]

The psychology of creative insight seems to follow a progression that begins with a conscious perplexity about the problem, followed by a period where it recedes from conscious thought, sinking into the fertile underground layers of the mind. There the unconscious appraises one solution after another until it hits upon something that may be the answer, pushing it upwards into consciousness as that sudden and spontaneous insight.

In 1869, the Russian chemist Dmitri Mendeleev, who had been working for years to discover a way of classifying the elements according to their atomic weight, fell into an exhausted sleep after devoting long hours to the problem. Later that night, Mendeleev, 'saw in a dream a table where all the elements fell into place as required'.[13] On waking, he immediately wrote down the table just as he remembered it in his dream. An amazed Mendeleev reported, 'Only in one place did a correction later seem necessary.' This was the genesis of the periodic table of elements, a fundamental discovery of modern chemistry.

Srinivasa Ramanujan, a self-taught maths prodigy

from India, rose from obscurity to being recognized as one of the greatest geniuses of the twentieth century. For him these dream insights were represented by the Goddess that came to him in his dreams presenting him with complex mathematical formulas which he would test and verify upon waking up. One such example was the infinite series for Pi.

The freedom fighter dreams of non-violent resistance, the scientist of his laboratory experiments, and the poet, Samuel Taylor Coleridge (1772–1834) dreamt the poem 'Kubla Khan' in full and finished form one lazy summer afternoon in his English countryside cottage.

He was turning the pages of a history book called *Purchas, His Pilgrimage*, in which he read the words, 'Here the Khan Kubla commanded a palace to be built…' Addicted to opium, he fell asleep. Three hours later when he awoke, the stately passages of 'Kubla Khan', no less than 'two to three hundred lines', were firmly in his mind. He seized pen, ink and paper and began writing. Unfortunately, no sooner had he begun than a person on business intruded and detained him for over an hour, so that, much to his mortification, except for the fifty-four lines we know today 'all the rest had passed away like the images on the surface of a stream into which a stone has been cast'. However, what remains of Coleridge's masterpiece is still soaked in the inspiration of his dream state, where he 'had drunk the milk of Paradise' so that the poem is still 'a miracle of rare device'.

Robert Louis Stevenson, the British author, had long been attempting to pen a story on man's dual nature, how the irrational side can overwhelm the mind. Dissatisfied with an earlier manuscript on this topic, he had destroyed it. Pressed for money, he resumed thinking about the theme: 'For two days I went about racking my brains for a plot of any sort; and on the second night I dreamed the scene at the window, and a scene afterward spilt in two, in which Hyde, pursued for some crime, took the powder and underwent the change in the presence of his pursuers. All the rest was made awake, and consciously, although I think I can trace in much of it the manner of my Brownies.'[14]

Stevenson's 'Brownies' were the little people of his dreams who would 'bestir themselves...and labour all night long' to produce 'truncheons of tales upon their lighted theatre' of the night.[15] So real were the dream-Brownies that according to him 'they can tell him a story piece by piece, like a serial, and keep him all the while in ignorance of where they aim'. He confessed that they gave him 'better tales than he could fashion for himself'.[16]

Charlotte Bronte, whose novels contain perfect descriptions of mental states she possibly could not have experienced owing to the restrictive circumstances that women of her time lived in, took the aid of her dreams to do so. Her description of an opium-induced state in *Villette* is so startlingly true to life that she was questioned if she had ever taken opium. Charlotte Bronte replied 'that she had never, to her knowledge, taken a grain of it in any shape, but that she had followed the process she always adopted when she had to describe anything which had not fallen within her own experience; she had thought intently on it for many and many a night before falling to sleep—wondering what it was like, or how it would be—till at length, sometimes after the progress of her story had been arrested at this one point for weeks, she awakened in the morning with all clear before her, as if she had in reality gone through the experience, and then could describe it, word for word, as it had happened'.[17] Charlotte Bronte seemed to have unwittingly followed what the ancient Greeks called incubating a dream—the sought dream.

Among present-day writers who have been inspired by dreams is Isabel Allende. In a Discovery Channel show entitled 'The Power of Dreams' (aired in 1994), she talked of how she had been struggling with the end of a story that she was working on when she had a dream that roused her creative imagination. She dreamt that she was sitting in a room with black furniture beside the corpse of her grandfather, draped in black, telling him about the book she had written. These images inspired her to conclude the story of her family's life with the grandfather's passing; it was as if she were keeping vigil by his body, waiting for the moment when she would bury him.[18] This was her bestselling debut novel *The House of Spirits*.

Among other writers who have claimed their work was inspired at times by their dreams are names like Sir Walter Scott, John Keats, Mark Twain, Edgar Alan Poe, H.G. Wells, Katherine Mansfield, Graham Greene and J.B. Priestly.

Writers, musicians, painters, performers seem much closer to the workings of the unconscious, instinctively realizing that it is the fount from which creativity springs. The famous painter Salvador Dali's fascination with dreams was stimulated after he read Freud's *Interpretation of Dreams*. Like some other surrealists, Dali attempted to preserve dream imagery on canvas, referring to his works as 'hand-painted dream photographs'.

The painter draws 'still' pictures while the film-maker produces moving visual images, sharing a commonality with dreams. Films, like dreams, change characters and setting, have flashbacks, can produce time distortions and yet project a reality. Ingmar Bergman, the well-known Swedish film-maker, who reproduced episodes from his dreams as accurately as possible in films such as *Naked Night* and *Wild Strawberries*, once said in an interview, 'I discovered that all my pictures were dreams. Of course I understood that some of my films were dreams, that part of them were dreams...but that all my pictures were dreams was a new discovery.'[19]

Dream creativity is not restricted only to mental enigmas or artistic inspirations. Jack Nicklaus, the famous golfer, saw the solution to a problematic golf swing in a dream. After winning a number of championships, he found himself in an embarrassing slump. When he regained his championship form seemingly overnight, a reporter from the *San Francisco Chronicle* (June 27, 1964) asked him how he had done it. He replied, 'I've been trying everything to find out what had been wrong... But last Wednesday night I had a dream and it was about my golf swing. I was hitting them pretty good in the dream and all at once I realized I wasn't holding the club the way I've actually been holding it lately. I've been having trouble collapsing my right arm taking the club head away from the ball, but I was doing it perfectly in my sleep. So when I came to the course yesterday morning, I tried it the way I did in my dream and it worked... I feel kind of foolish admitting it, but it really happened in a dream.'[20]

Why didn't this dream come to Nicklaus earlier? Why did it wait till his game was in a slump? Had Banting received his instructions in a dream ten, or fifteen years earlier, wouldn't many more people have been saved the suffering inflicted by diabetes?

Let's ask if these people were prepared to heed their dreams had they come earlier. When Nicklaus was winning tournament after tournament would he have paid attention to a 'silly' dream commenting on his swing? Probably not. But the dreamer may certainly be tempted to try the dream's instructions if he or she has been grappling with the problem for a long time and has exhausted all consciously reasoned avenues. Questions like these are of great interest to researchers while they study the 'why' and 'how' of creativity. In fact, the process behind dream insights noted earlier resembles the well-known steps of the creative process itself—both being inexorably linked to the unconscious.

We ordinary dreamers—those of us who are not novelists, scientists, musicians and inventors—can also use dreams for solving problems in our everyday lives. Twenty-three-year-old Sangeeta Kaul, who was developing a computerized network of libraries (Delnet) at the India International Centre in Delhi, recounted that while working on a particular software program, she was unable to access one particular section of it. She wanted information on how many libraries accessed her company's data. For three months she had tried but could not find the right command. Then one night she dreamt of the command that would execute the program. Even in the dream, she knew that the command was the right one. Sangeeta was at her office at seven-thirty next morning. She punched in her dream-dictated command and, sure enough, it worked.

'Nita Berry' writes books for children. While holidaying in Goa she was horrified at the extent of pollution of the sea by industrial waste. The fish fed on the waste gradually became resistant to it, and the catch when sold in the markets had harmful toxic effects on those who ate the fish. Deeply troubled by the issue and wishing to write a story around it, she fell asleep. Quite like Stevenson, Nita's little Brownies set to work and she dreamt the entire plot of her story. Nita awoke from her dream drama and in one continuous stretch wrote the story out—a story that won her India's prestigious Shankar's Award.

In the tough world of business and management, Dr Francis Menezes—director of the Tata Management Training Institute, Pune—put the creativity of the dreaming mind to one of the most striking uses. His pioneering dream workshops at the Institute aim at stimulating creativity and at problem-solving through dreams.

Curious to know how he was introducing the romantic world of dreams to the hard-nosed realm of business, I went to Pune to meet him. Over forty engineers and corporate and management executives, had come to attend Menezes's workshop. After dinner Menezes, a frail man with a disarmingly gentle smile, ushered us into a large room where he spoke about the power of the unconscious to solve knotty interpersonal problems, enhance performance and provide a new impetus in accomplishing goals.

He said, 'I am not here to ply you with dream theories, but I want you to do one thing tonight. Take a piece of paper and think of a problem that has been bothering you. It may be a work problem or an interpersonal dilemma. In a single-phrase question, write it down, insert the paper into an envelope, and put it under your pillow. Just before going to sleep, ponder over your question. When you wake up the next morning try and remember your dream, and write it down immediately. We will then see what the problem and its solution are.'

'Single-phrase questions' could be: Why am I stuck in my project? How do I redesign the machine I am working on? Why is it so difficult to get along with my boss? How do I quit smoking?

A somewhat bemused gathering of executives left the room that night. They had expected talks on motivation and how to enhance their creativity. They had not expected to be told to go to their rooms and dream!

Within the space of a three-day workshop, he said, he opened the way for over seventy per cent of the participants to tap into their own resources to find solutions to their dilemmas, instead of relying on imposed ones. You may notice that Menezes's programme followed a certain order that many creative dreamers had followed unwittingly. He led the participants through the process of deliberate immersion by asking them to focus clearly and single-mindedly on an issue for which they wanted an answer. Writing it down and putting it under the pillow was a way of 'priming the pump' for the process of incubation to take place during sleep.

Breakthrough Dreams

Menezes demonstrated the efficacy of his programme when he was hired by a gigantic chemical manufacturing firm owned by the Government of India to solve a morale problem in its Research and Development wing. He invited fifty-two scientists from the department to spend three days and nights at Pune. Each evening, after dinner, he asked the scientists to think of a persistent, nagging workplace problem, then write it down in a single phrase and think about it before going to sleep.

The results were startling. After the first night each of the scientists, including the sceptics, announced that they had dreamt surprisingly relevant dreams about their work-related problems. One scientist, for instance, found himself haranguing one of his most competent co-workers; another scientist found himself pelting his unappreciative boss with lab equipment! Based on the analysis of the dreams, Menezes suggested his recommendations to the firm's top brass. Dreams of a large number of the participants revealed that they were working in an atmosphere of fear and suspicion. So impressed was the management that they initiated a number of changes—better internal communication, productive teamwork and more flexible working conditions.

Perhaps more impressive was the fact that independent of the workplace, most of the participants in the dream workshops sustained it as an ongoing process, and started their own weekly meetings to discuss their dreams and review the week's outcome.

The real power of dreams lies in their ability to change our habitual way of looking at the world. A child's vivid imagination and unjaded curiosity sees the world as full of mystery and wonder. The older we grow, originality and creativity are smothered by the stubborn forces of custom and conditioning, by environmental, social and educational determinants. The order and discipline of conventional thought stultifies the fluidity of thought and perception and the ability to discern new patterns, spot interesting analogies and make insightful leaps.

Luckily our dreams remain untainted; they are spontaneous and autonomous expressions that combine elements in extraordinary ways, see correspondences and connections where none existed before and which may point out close links to our waking concerns. In each of the dreams discussed above none of the images were random or bizarre, but had specific relevance to the dreamer's preoccupation. Each dreamer was able to see the dream images as an answer to their waking concern, like the snakes in Kekule's dream.

It is noteworthy that in these varied examples the dreams are taken literally. There seems no question of looking for any hidden significance in the dream images. Howe's dream had all the symbolic imagery to unravel it within a psychological framework. A tribe of spear-wielding savages leading a hapless victim to death could be treated by a Freudian therapist as an expression of the uprising of the primitive sexual (spears) urge by whose sway the dreamer feared being overwhelmed. Stevenson's dream of Hyde being pursued for a crime and changing his persona in the presence of his pursuers may be interpreted as the 'splitting' of the many selves that reside within us, depending upon circumstantial provocation. Bohr's dream of horses running in lanes that were clearly marked by white dust, which if transgressed disqualified the horse, even though couched in metaphorical language, was not interpreted by him as a psychological truth. For all these dreamers the dreams were not symbolic commentaries on their psychological state; they were taken literally and granted the same validity as any significant waking perception.

Had these dreamers not recalled their dream, reality would have remained unchanged. The dream became the cause of the outer event. It then becomes difficult to define which half of the experience is more significant: the dream as the dark womb that seeds the idea, or wakefulness that nourishes its growth.

It is important to distinguish these dreams from those that simply reveal an event about to happen: the precognitive dream that reflects a future event, without being its cause. With or without the dream the event was bound to happen. The rationalist may well ask: How can you hear the echo before the sound? However, it is worth pointing out that both these dream types—those that can reflect reality and those that can change it—remain outside the realm of the ordinary dream. Occasionally, a dream makes such a strong impact that its vividness is remembered long after, allowing the dreamer to speculate that the dream may, after all, cause or reflect reality.

Needless to say that millions of diabetics are grateful that Banting's belief did change reality.

10. The Sentinels of the Body—Illness and Healing Dreams

We have seen that dreams are often affected by the experiences of the previous day. Sometimes outside events when we are asleep find expression in a dream. The oft-quoted example is of the alarm clock triggering a dream of church bells ringing. If for some reason the bed has become cold and damp it may be experienced as drowning in an icy sea; if warm, an inferno. A peal of thunder may set us amidst battle; the creaking of a door may produce a dream of burglars; and if our head happens to be buried under the pillow, we may dream of being beneath a huge, overhanging rock.

If the stimulus, instead of coming from an external source, comes from an internal organ of our body, can it trigger a dream? The philosopher Schopenhauer argued that during the day the mind is totally occupied with external stimuli, so that any stimulus coming from within the body is all but drowned. But at night when the deafening impressions of the day are mute, our attention may be attracted by stimuli emanating from the organs—just like at night we can hear the murmuring of a brook that is drowned by daytime noise. Thus, can a change in the respiratory rate lead to dreams of suffocation or drowning; changes in the ear trigger a dream of a shouting demagogue? Can imperceptible bodily fluctuations register in our dreams? If so, it would mean that dreams can become a barometer of changes taking place in the body.

From here it is only a small step to the belief that dreams can warn us of impending illness, as also of recovery from them. In fact, when the harmony in the body is disturbed, perhaps our dreams may often be the first to know. Internal organs may register indistinctly when we are in a healthy state. However, when they are malfunctioning, they can send more urgent intimations.

A poignant case is of a woman, three months pregnant, who dreamt that much to her horror her green carpet had turned red. Next day she began to haemorrhage and lost her child. Was the dream warning her that green, the colour of life and growth had transformed to the colour of blood?

In another instance, 'Mandira Mukerjee' dreamt:

> *I'm driving my car and suddenly realize that I have run out of fuel. I find myself stranded in a remote village.*

Five days later, quite unexpectedly, Mandira's blood pressure dropped and she was advised complete rest. The car, a symbol of her body, is brought to a sudden halt as it ran out of fuel. The feeling of being stranded in the dream is a metaphor for her inability to temporarily lead a normal life.

It may be argued that the above two dreams presaged future occurrences and were not necessarily dreams that recorded subtle changes in the body.

But then isn't it a common experience to eat a scrumptious meal in a dream and then wake up to find yourself ravenously hungry? Did the dream cause the feelings of hunger, or was your stomach experiencing hunger pangs while you were asleep and these sensations triggered the dream of food?

The dream viewed as a diagnostic tool that monitors our health was an idea I wanted to explore further and cross-check with medical doctors. I met over a dozen of them but their responses ranged from downright disbelief to amusement and condescension. 'How can dreams tell you about illnesses? Only physical examination and tests can do that. Nothing else.'

Then I met Dr 'Trehan', a surgeon at Apollo Hospital in Delhi, who at least seemed interested in discussing the subject. 'Well, I have had some rather inexplicable things happen to me, some rather unusual responses from people I am treating.'

'In what way?'

'Twice, patients have recounted conversations to me I'd had either with a colleague or an assistant while operating on them. How could they have known?' Dr Trehan shook his head in perplexity.

'We probably have other ways of "knowing",' I ventured.

'Maybe. Both of them told me that they had floated up to the ceiling, from where they had observed the operation and had heard everything.' His eyes travelled towards the ceiling. 'I didn't quiz them but I have never forgotten them.

'Then there was another man—a simple, rather poor

man—who told me he had seen me in a dream and insisted that only I should operate on him. It did occur to me that it was a very clever way of pressurizing me. Then he looked at me and asked, "You do not believe me, do you?" "How can I?" I said to him. The man shook his head and said, "In the dream you also told me the date."

'It was a month away. I smiled, checked my appointment diary, and gave him a date fourteen days hence for his operation. I said to him, "Well, you may have seen my face in a dream but you have got the dates all wrong. I'll operate on you—dream or no dream."

'Then something odd happened. I fell ill and did not go to work for a week. My appointments had to be rescheduled, and this man's operation had to be postponed. Two days before the operation, he was admitted into the hospital for pre-operative care. I checked in on him on my rounds. The first thing he said was, "My dream was true. Day after will be exactly a month since I met you."'

'Do you now believe that he saw your face in a dream?' I asked Dr Trehan.

'He may have. But since I cannot find a reasonable explanation for it, I continue to be semi-sceptical.'

I felt his anecdotes didn't quite fit what I was looking for. 'Have any of your other patients ever mentioned a dream that may have provided a clue for the onset of their illness?'

Dr Trehan asked me to accompany him to the ward and talk to any of the patients who were willing. Needless to say, most of the patients were not interested in what I had to say. They looked at me disbelievingly when I told them that I was neither a physiotherapist or a nutrition expert, nor a doctor assisting Dr Trehan, but a person researching dreams! Their expressions seemed to say, 'We are in hospital to be cured, not to dream!' However, a girl in her late twenties seemed interested. Her large eyes followed me keenly. 'Pushpa Bansal' was just twenty-five when her troubles began with persistent headaches. She remembered a dream from that period, which she related within minutes of our introduction:

> *I am in a computer factory where small fires are flaring up from the walls and leaping out in threatening clusters from the centre of the factory. I'm trying to get out but the workers in the factory are not letting me.*

This dream depicts her condition faithfully. The brain has often been compared to a computer and the fires could represent her headaches. Her desire to 'get out' is probably indicative of the effort she was making not to let her headaches bog her down. She appears not to have succeeded—the workers in the factory, or the cells in her brain, are not operating normally, and holding her ransom to the dysfunction. Admittedly, I was looking for these correlations.

The passage of months saw her condition deteriorate; the headaches became more and more intense with sharp pains shooting down her neck. One day, while watching television, she fainted. When she came round, she began to throw up. She was rushed to hospital where medication controlled the vomiting, but a dull headache still persisted. The doctors suspected a tumour in the brain, but a confirmed diagnosis could not be given till a CT scan was done.

Illness and Healing Dreams

Nobody had told Pushpa about the suspicion of a tumour, but she had overheard her parents whispering to each other. Surprisingly, she was concerned more for them than her own condition. However, everyone maintained an optimistic facade, chatting about everything except the one subject uppermost in their minds. This secrecy was perhaps what made her open up to me so quickly. I was a stranger with whom no pretences were required, and she obviously needed to talk. She remembered a dream from the previous night, which she excitedly related to me:

> *I have been given a large watermelon. I cut it open to find, to my utter amazement, that it is seedless! I shape it in the form of a lotus.*

'Is it a good dream?' she asked, and then continued before I could answer: 'After all, the lotus is a sacred flower. Maybe if I pray God may make me well.'

I didn't know what to say. It isn't uncommon to have wish-fulfilment dreams when you are confronted with the prospect of a life-threatening illness. Yet I felt there was something strange about the dream. Watermelons are full of seeds but this one is seedless. I felt that this could be the lead metaphor of the dream. However, try as I would, I could not interpret the dream beyond this initial observation. Perhaps my concern made her continue to chat with me.

'When is the CT scan?' I asked.

'Tomorrow.'

Two days later Pushpa still filled my thoughts. She had looked so bewildered and lost, yet so utterly brave in her struggle not to let despair overwhelm her.

On the third day I was back at the hospital, but Pushpa's bed was empty. I was worried and wondered if she was already in the OT. I went to see Dr Trehan.

'Oh, Pushpa!' he exclaimed. 'She has been discharged. Her CT scan was clear of any kind of tumour. Her problem was traced to excessive water retention in the brain.'

As I walked out of the hospital my mind went back to Pushpa's dream. The watermelon could be taken as a symbol for the brain—its globular shape similar to that of the brain. It was seedless. A tumour would have appeared like a black shadow in the CT scan, akin to the seeds of a watermelon. No tumours, the dream seemed to be telling Pushpa!

The dream's choice of symbol was truly amazing. Perhaps it pointed towards a prognosis as well. A watermelon retains water and the lotus grows in water. Could it be that both alluded to the problem of water retention that Pushpa was facing? In the dream she shapes the watermelon into a lotus—a positive symbol of healing, since the lotus lives and thrives in water without being swamped by it.

Once the problem was diagnosed, the doctors prescribed the right drug to dry the excessive fluid in Pushpa's brain. Pushpa got her life back and I was beginning to see that dreams could be a voice for our body. No doubt Pushpa's dream found its interpretation after the event. But what was amazing was that the dream imagery was actually like a CT scan.

It is unfortunate that the notion that dreams can warn the dreamer about impending illness has not been explored in modern times. Scientific researchers are all too keen to study the effects of biochemical and physiological factors on dreaming, but the influence of malfunctioning organs on the content of dreams is not considered. Also, there is hardly any literature available on this aspect of dreaming.

Fortunately, Russian psychiatrist Vasily Kasatkin, at the Leningrad Neurosurgical Institute, had not disregarded the somatic basis of dreaming. His book, *A Theory of Dreams* (1967), relied on the most comprehensive research on the relationship between dreams and bodily ailments, and described his findings based on 10,240 dreams obtained from twelve hundred subjects over a span of forty years. Kasatkin felt dreams were not about our psychology—the dominant view nowadays—but that their images derived from stimuli within the body. Accordingly, he asked people to note their health, environmental conditions like temperature, and the sensations felt in various parts of their body when recording their dreams.

Kasatkin discusses at length the types of dreams associated with illness. An increased dream recall is associated with illness, and these dreams are longer than those caused by minor annoyances. In general, dreams announcing illnesses were distressful and included violent images of war, fire, blood, corpses, tombs, raw meat, garbage, dirty water, spoiled food or references to hospitals, doctors and medicines. Though these dreams were gloomy and frightening, pain was seldom experienced. Changes in dream content began occurring shortly before the onset of an illness or the appearance of any clinical symptoms of the disorder, and these dreams paralleled the course of the disease. As symptoms worsened, so did the dream content; as the symptoms abated, the dream images grew less unpleasant.

One of Kasatkin's most dramatic conclusions was that in almost every case, the patient's dream images involved the appearance of the affected organ or body part, indicating its location, the sensation it undergoes, and its malfunctioning. Patricia Garfield confirmed this in her book *The Healing Power of Dreams*, where she says our dreams even reflect the onset of something as ordinary as a headache. 'I have examined over forty dream reports from people who awoke with headaches they did not have before they went to sleep—some from my own collection of people's dreams, others from research studies.' In various dream images leading up to headaches, the dreamer is hit on the head either with an axe by an assailant, or with books, or by falling material as a building collapses. Garfield stresses that in each of the dream images the sense of violence to the head is prominent.

Kasatkin came to believe that recurrent dreams of bodily wounds 'are amongst the most serious and they invariably indicate a very dangerous illness such as cancer, liver trouble, kidney or heart disease'. For instance, repeated dreams of a chest wound are indicative of a possible heart attack. Recurrent dreams of stomach wounds may suggest liver or kidney disease. He reported the case of a forty-year-old man who had a recurrent dream of a rat gnawing at the lower part of his abdomen and was later diagnosed with a duodenal ulcer.[1]

Kasatkin called dreams the 'sentries that watch over our health. There are nerves coming to the brain from every part of the body—and they relay the signals of impending illness that the subconscious translates into dreams'.

He wanted to develop a system of early warning of

disease through dreams, especially for people who had recurrent dreams about a specific body part. Numerous reports of dreams preceding the onset of cancer have been published. 'One author traces links between dreams, disturbing emotions, lowered functioning of the immune system, and increased susceptibility to cancer. He claims that the images in dreams can symbolize the type of cancer and its location and gives the example of a woman who had recurrent nightmares of dogs tearing at her stomach a few months before she was diagnosed with stomach cancer.'[2]

Bernard Siegel, a cancer surgeon at the Yale University School of Medicine, described the case of a journalist who had a dream in which torturers placed burning hot coals beneath his chin. He felt the heat sear his throat and screamed in pain as the 'coals gnawed his larynx'. The journalist felt sure that this dream indicated some malfunction in his throat even though he had a tough time persuading his doctor to take him seriously. A physical check confirmed the presence of cancer in his thyroid gland.[3]

Kasatkin was interviewed by two American writers for the *National Enquirer* in 1975. Under a bold front-page headline declaring 'Dreams Are Saving Lives', the article quoted Kasatkin: 'By correctly interpreting dreams we've been able to discover and treat serious illnesses long before they could be diagnosed by any traditional means. We have been able to save many lives.'

His dream diagnoses covered a wide range of diseases from minor tooth and skin problems to brain tumours. Kasatkin felt that the time-span between a dream and the actual appearance of the disease varied. He noted it might be two weeks for a heart attack and a year or more for the manifestation of mental illness.

A definite connection seems to exist between the condition of our bodies and what appears on the monitoring screen of our dreaming mind. This idea has ancient roots in history and has been practised by many civilizations with very effective results. In Greece, the cult of the healing god Aesculapius flourished for nearly a thousand years, from the end of the sixth century BCE until the end of the fifth century CE. People thronged from all over to these temples to seek cures for ailments. Dream incubation, or the art of inducing specific dreams became a highly developed art with the Greeks. People, after sacramental ceremonies and purification rites in the temples, would drift into sleep with a question in their mind. Once asleep they would dream of the remedies for their illness. These dreams, interpreted by the priests, would reveal the cure. Similar practices also took place in some Hindu temples, for example, the Shiva temple at Tarakeswar (in West Bengal, India).

What I am suggesting through this is that it is important to notice when dreams deviate from their normal expression. The dream is drawing attention to sensations that are still too feeble to register as symptoms in the body. For example, these changes could express themselves as dream images that depict transformations in nature: the sun drying the earth could signify inflammation or fever; a cold air blowing through the window, turning the house and garden into ice and snow sculptures, could indicate an excess of white phlegm or poor blood circulation. The nature of the imagery becomes the indicator of the specific organ that is under siege.

Illness and Healing Dreams

The ancient Greek physicians called this a *prodromal* dream, from the Greek word *pro* meaning 'before' and *dromos* meaning 'running', thus, a forerunner. Today 'prodrome' in medical terminology refers to a symptom—an indicator of the onset of a disease.

The Hindu-Buddhist genius for classifying ideas or theories becomes evident when dealing with these dreams. The sixty-eighth appendix of the *Atharvaveda* states that human beings dream according to a specific individual pattern. Current research has confirmed that indeed the dreaming pattern of people does not vary much over the years. The Hindus further state that this pattern conforms to the temperament of the person.

This is not only a method of classifying dreams according to the temperament of the dreamer, but it can also reflect the psychosomatic condition of the dreamer. For example, when a particular bodily sense is disturbed, the dreamer will dream of objects of that sense.[4] This could be of immense significance when diagnosing the health of the person through dreams. Indian medical texts go on to make much more specific diagnoses based on dreams. Dreaming of friendship with a dog means that the dreamer will become feverish; friendship with a monkey, consumptive; friendship with a demon, insane; friendship with ghosts, amnesiac.[5] Similarly, according to Vaisesika philosophers, a man may dream of flying when wind predominates his body.[6]

It may be relevant to point out that homoeopathy also seeks to understand and embed the symptoms of a patient guided by his or her dreams.[7]

Besides warning us about imminent illnesses, dreams

signal our return to health as well. Slowly, among the unpleasant images of loss, impairment and weakness, new elements arise. Although negative dream content may continue for some time, positive images signal the beginning of our return to health. The two may intermingle for a while.

Those who have undergone surgery may have dreams of meat being chopped, or blood oozing—a symbolic depiction of surgery. Immediately after a hysterectomy a woman dreamt of being raped by strangers, characterizing the sense of violence inflicted on the body. However, within these violent dreams a different image may occur indicating recovery. Hippocrates put it succinctly: 'New objects indicate a change.'[8]

'Manjula Mehra' too had a radical hysterectomy to contend with. She also underwent two cycles of chemotherapy. Six months later, when she was due for her cancer marker test, which would determine whether the cancer had been arrested or not, she had the following dream:

> *Some ruffians are chasing me and I'm running to save myself. The ruffians overtake me and pull at the shawl I'm wearing. The tug-of-war is so intense that at one point I feel I've lost the battle. Suddenly, I manage to extricate myself and escape. A great sense of relief floods me as I look at the shawl and find that it is totally intact. I had feared it would be torn or damaged, but it is whole and in one piece.*

The shawl symbolizes Manjula's body (many religions refer to the body as the raiment or clothing of the soul) which is being ravaged by ruffians, like the cancer ravaging her body. The initial part of the dream relives the trauma of the invasion of cancer and surgery from which she tried to escape. The tug-of-war was intense and at times she felt she had lost the battle.

Be it rape, or ruffians violating the integrity of the body in the case of Manjula, such dreams contain powerful symbols of what these women felt and had to come to terms with. In Manjula's case, however, in spite of her encounter with the ruffians, or cancer, the shawl or the body is intact. The symbols of wholeness, of lack of damage, are embedded within the dream as pointers towards healing. Despite the earlier ravages, the dream reassured her that her body was moving towards recovery.

A few days later, the cancer tests confirmed this. The cancer marker in her blood had dropped from 390 to 10 (30 is considered the normal count). As Manjula said, 'The confirmation of this dream brought the bounce back into my step.'

11. Seriously Strange: The Paranormal Dream

When Rajeev and I were living in the ashram, I had once quite casually related a dream to a friend. I was in Oxford, walking along a covered area that looked into a library. I had vividly described the books and the tables on which people were reading, and ended by saying that, perhaps, the dream mirrored my desire to study in Oxford. My friend, who had graduated from Oxford, was startled. The dream, she felt, had quite accurately described the Bodleian Library, as though I had actually seen it. Since I had never travelled overseas at the time, nor did I have any memory of ever seeing a photograph of the library, what exactly had transpired? Had I travelled there 'astrally' to be able to describe it? Was it sheer coincidence? Or had my description triggered an association in my friend's mind, conflating memory with image?

Many years later I did go to Oxford, and, needless to say, one of the first places I visited was the Bodleian Library. I was stunned—my dream had captured the essence of what my eyes beheld now. No doubt it was not identical; the dream images were superimposed with elements that I can only call projective content. So it was a half-and-half situation, which neither allows the dream to be dismissed as 'illusion', nor confirms it as 'astral travel'.

The protagonists for paranormal dreaming, and there are many, would contend that the dream was casting a glance towards the future, merely alerting me sixteen years earlier that one day I would visit Oxford.

This dimension to dreams suggests a non-ordinary vista of perception that is very challenging. The fact was that, coincidence or not, I had been able to describe something that existed in real time without ever having visited it and, more importantly, someone familiar with it was able to identify it as such.

Another example may prove illustrative in a different way. This dream is from the files of the Jungian psychotherapist Marie-Louise von Franz.[1] A domineering woman with a very strong power complex dreamt of three tigers seated threateningly in front of her. Her analyst counselled her that the dream was indicative of her devouring attitude towards other people, as symbolized by the three tigers. Given the personality of the dreamer it seemed a very apt interpretation. But for the fact that the dreamer and her friend strolling along Lake Zurich later that very afternoon noticed a crowd gathered near a barn. Curious, they ventured nearer. The lady was shocked to see three tigers sitting in a row, exactly as in her dream! Now can we be sure that the psychological interpretation of the dream encompasses the full intent of the dreaming mind? Could not the dream also have been informing our domineering woman of sighting something unusual the next day? After all, it's perhaps rare even in an Indian jungle to witness three tigers sitting together in a row—and this was Switzerland! (The tigers were part of a circus spending the night in town.)

Sceptics will point out that though the event matched the dream in the above cases, in hundreds of instances there is no outcome to attest the dream episode. Then why are we ready to give a precognitive dimension to such dream events? I do not pretend to have the answers, but we will explore this aspect of dreams in greater depth.

Belief in and the acceptance of precognitive and other paranormal phenomena has been widespread since the earliest recorded times. Existential enquiries indicative of the supernatural were the purview of religious teachings. In fact the *Atharvaveda* and other Indian texts suggest a connection between the time of night when a prophetic dream has occurred and its possible time of fulfilment. A dream from the first quarter of sleep will come true within a year, the dreams arising in the second quarter of the night within eight months, those from the third quarter within three months, and the dreams that come in the last part of sleep, or early morning, are indicative of events that have already been set in motion.[2]

In *Timaeus*, Plato defines the state conducive for precognition: 'No man, when in his wits, attains prophetic truth and inspiration; but when he receives the inspired word, either his intelligence is enthralled in sleep, or he is demented by some distemper or possession.'

The ability to 'sense' the future is not uncommon. In one study, questionnaires were given to approximately 2,500 eighth-grade students in northern India, 200 university students in West Africa, and 300 students at the University of Virginia, in the US, asking them if they had ever had paranormal dreams. About one out of every six of the eighth-grade students and one out of every three of the university students indicated that they had experienced a paranormal dream at some time during their life.

Perhaps 'knowing' may have wider gateways and thresholds of perception than just the five senses. To borrow from Hamlet, 'there are more things in heaven and earth, Horatio, than are dreamt of in your philosophy'.

Here are a few dreams that gave to the dreamer a peephole into the future. 'Rahul Verma' was studying for his engineering examination. Late at night he put his books aside and went to sleep. Here's what he dreamt:

> I'm sitting in the examination hall and the invigilator hands me the question paper. I read through the ten questions listed there and debate which one to tackle first.

The following day Rahul was stunned when the same ten questions appeared in the exam paper handed to him by the invigilator. This is not an isolated case; I've had many similar accounts related to me, including one from a retired Chief Justice of the Supreme Court of India.

'Susan Verghese' works at Lyon's Hospital in Delhi. Previously, she had worked at the Methodist hospital at Madurai. Once on night duty, exhausted after the day's rush of activity, Susan was overcome by sleep. At about four o'clock in the morning she told the other two nurses that she needed to take a short nap. She then dreamt:

> I see a patient being rushed into the emergency, with severe bleeding from the mouth. The man has a dark, thin, long face and I feel I need to attend to him immediately.

Susan awoke from the dream, automatically put on her cap and glided silently through the dimmed corridors of the hospital towards the emergency ward, even though her night duty was in the general wards. To her amazement, she was confronted with the same dark, thin, long face she had just seen in her dream, being rushed into the emergency. It was a case of severe bleeding from a rare gum infection and a nurse who had dealt with such a patient before was needed for the surgery. None of the nurses, with the exception of Susan, were familiar with this kind of infection. And there stood Susan, assisting in the dressing, wondering at the unreality of it all, at the strange synchronicity of the dream, the patient, and her arrival just when and where she was needed. Years later she still continues to wonder about this unknown face that had unwittingly propelled her into the emergency ward: How did I see this man through walls, darkness and closed eyelids? What power made me walk straight to where I was needed?

Yes, what power is it within us that not only directed Susan to where she was needed, but can also—as in the following case—accurately predict the date of one's death? However incredible it might seem, it happened to my husband's grandfather, Balraj Bhalla. He noted a dream in his diary in June 1956, which he also mentioned to his wife:

> *I am reading the newspaper. I turn to the section on obituaries and read, 'Balraj Bhalla died on the 25th of December 1956. The prayer ceremony will be at 3 pm on...'*

The Paranormal Dream

As his dream had foretold, six months later, Balraj Bhalla died on Christmas day. Was it a fantastic coincidence or did something within him 'know', and found its voice within a dream?

Balraj Bhalla is not an isolated case of foreknowledge of death. Keki Daruwalla, the poet and writer, recounts that his wife awoke one morning from a very disturbing dream. In the dream she saw Keki, their grandchild and herself involved in a terrible road accident near traffic lights.

Keki and his wife were due to go to the US to meet their daughter and grandchild, and Mrs Daruwalla was looking forward to the visit. However, as the date for departure came closer, an inexplicable reluctance to go seized her, so much so that she wanted to cancel the trip. But finally she dismissed her forebodings and they decided to go ahead with their plans. Four months after her dream, Keki was driving the car with Mrs Daruwalla beside him in the streets of Austin, Texas. Just as they approached a traffic signal, a speeding paramedic pick-up hit their car broadside with great force.

Mrs Daruwalla died in the accident. Unlike the events in the dream, their granddaughter was not in the car. In hindsight Mrs Daruwalla's reluctance to go abroad was not unfounded. Contrary to everything else that suggested a pleasant trip, she had a strong premonition of what would happen. Uncannily, her dream had depicted the manner of her death.

Anyone who has experienced a predictive dream that has come true is staunchly convinced about precognition. If one was to suggest to them that what happened was a mere coincidence and that their dreams held no foreknowledge of coming events, they would look at them with utter disbelief. They may not be clear about the hows and whys of it, nor about its philosophical implications, but they do not doubt its reality. A small incident happened to my husband Rajeev on his way to catch a train from Delhi to Jalandhar. He was running late, and there was the usual traffic jam at the entrance to New Delhi Railway Station. With his small overnighter, he rushed to the platform to buy a ticket. As he wove his way through the throng of people, he suddenly remembered his dream of the previous night: *His bag has been stolen at New Delhi Railway Station.* He shrugged it aside as anxiety about the impending trip, but soon thereafter, he asked himself: What will I miss most if my bag is stolen?

The question remained unanswered, as he negotiated his way through the crowd. He reached the ticket counter and put his bag down beside him to pay for the ticket. Within the space of collecting the ticket and his hand reaching down to pick up the bag, it was gone. Stolen.

Later, Rajeev could only lament, 'If only I had paid attention...'

Was it an anxiety dream, or a nocturnal prompting warning him to be careful? In hindsight, its precognitive content is difficult to deny.

Despite the widespread prevalence of paranormal dreams, a deep scepticism about them prevails in the modern mind. There is no denying that there are some inherent difficulties with respect to explaining paranormal dreams in general and in precognition in particular. Our reservations primarily arise because most dreams are not prophetic. Moreover, the field of paranormal phenomena has had a long-standing association with people who are delusional. They exhibit paranormal tendencies like telepathy and the ability to make predictions about the future. However, these abilities disappear once the person regains mental health, suggesting that they were directly related to the person's delusional state. Therefore these accounts are considered unreliable. Adding to the burden of disbelief are accounts of normal people who for want of fame or attention invent episodes involving paranormal phenomena. Others who are not basically fraudulent, may unconsciously subject their genuine experiences to retrospective falsification. This last aspect is a rather subtle and complicated issue. Suppose a man dreams about his ageing father; when he awakes, his belief that his ailing father may not have long to live fastens onto the dream. Thus 'I dreamt about my ill father' may unwittingly transform into 'I dreamt that my father is dead'. And if the father does die soon afterwards, was the dream actually a precognition or was it retrospectively falsified? Since in most of these cases there is no intention to defraud, no useful purpose is served by highlighting the difference to the dreamer.

I suggested to Rajeev that he had retrospectively falsified his dream about his bag being stolen and that he may have experienced a simple anxiety dream with vivid images of the New Delhi Railway Station. And, perhaps, the next day the unbidden thought of losing his bag had got superimposed on the previous night's anxiety dream, leading him to believe he had had a precognitive dream. He conceded that this was a very alluring explanation. But, he countered, 'Granted, it may not have been a prophetic dream, but then how do you explain my thoughts just before the bag was stolen?'

At first glance this seems to be a remarkable coincidence. Or one may argue he may have subliminally noticed a warning against pick-pockets near the railway station and the unbidden thought had crossed Rajeev's mind as he neared the ticket counter.

We also have to contend with the issue as to whether a dream still qualifies as a prophetic dream if it does not predict the *exact* outcome. To illustrate: a man may dream that his ailing father died on the twelfth of September, and his father passes away on the ninth of December. Is the dream a hit or a miss? After all, the two dates—12/9 and 9/12—are transposable and liable to be muddled in the dream.

No doubt these reasons lead to ambiguity when confronted with paranormal phenomena. But this does not mean that we deny all paranormal incidents outright; it only cautions us not to be credulous.

Unlike in early times, when it was supposed that only a select few were gifted with this special power, it is now believed that ordinary people, in fact, the whole human race, has a latent extra-sensory power, which manifests most often through dreams. Since the nineteenth-century, researchers have been codifying such 'seeing'. These paranormal phenomena are now being distinguished into various types of extra-sensory abilities: clairvoyance, telepathy and precognition. Clairvoyance is the ability to see objects or events that by their remoteness in space or time cannot be seen by ordinary vision; telepathy is the ability to transmit and receive thoughts without recourse to any known form of communication; and in precognition information of the event is available prior to its occurrence. Precognition is different from both telepathy and clairvoyance as it alludes to foreknowledge—the event has yet to happen. It is like hearing the echo before the sound.

Vinay Mehta, the captain of a merchant vessel, had embarked on a voyage from Portland to Japan. It was a clear night as the ship sailed peacefully in the North Pacific Ocean. Captain Mehta came to the wheelhouse where he was smartly saluted by the second mate, who was on duty. The captain looked out into the night and noted with satisfaction that the visibility was good and the sky, sprayed with stars, was unclouded. He told the second mate that he was going down to his cabin to sleep.

While asleep, Captain Mehta dreamt that his ship was in grave danger and was about to crash into another ship. He awoke with a start and checked his watch. It was two-thirty in the morning. He looked out of his porthole to see the light of another ship nearby. Instantly, he realized the ship was too close and that they were on a collision course. He rushed to the wheelhouse to discover that the ship was on autopilot and the second mate was nowhere in sight. He disengaged the autopilot and changed the course of the ship, thereby preventing a major disaster. Needless to say, the second mate was charge-sheeted for dereliction of duty and signed off the vessel.

Dream clairvoyance was operating in Vinay Mehta's case, as also in Susan's experience of 'seeing' a man with a severe case of bleeding in the gums. Rahul Verma had also 'seen' the exam paper by 'second sight'.

In the case of telepathy, enough evidence has been accumulated to postulate some conditions that are conducive for it. It is now believed that telepathic dreams usually occur between persons closely bound to each other by strong emotional ties. Telepathy is normally accompanied by an event occurring in conditions that are adverse to communication, like geographical distance, helplessness, inhibition or repression. There must also be a need to overcome this barrier—which usually happens during sleep.

We have, however, not been able to identify any element of a dream that can alert us to its precognitive content. It seems that only in retrospect can we be sure that a dream is precognitive. Yet some people, like Balraj Bhalla and Mrs Daruwalla, felt uneasy when confronted with an unusually vivid dream.

This is not to suggest that precognitive dreams predominantly concern the death of someone or dwell on distress or danger. Both examples of precognition cited above are about death, and even the other dreams—Susan's and Vinay's—concern an emergency. Precognition may also focus on other matters too.

Is it possible that paranormal dreams can warn us about large-scale calamities? In surveys conducted of two different incidents people were questioned about precognitive warnings of an impending disaster. The first related to the tragic accident of the *Titanic*. Among the people questioned were those who had somehow not boarded the ill-fated ship. J. Connon Middleton, due to sail to New York on the *Titanic* for a business conference, for two nights in a row, dreamt of seeing the *Titanic* wrecked beyond redemption and seeing 'her passengers and crew swimming around her'. Deeply concerned, and feeling uneasy and oppressed, he told his friends and family about his dreams, but did not cancel his trip to America until a few days later when he received a cable from New York urging him to delay his journey and take passage on another ship.[3]

Colin MacDonald, a marine engineer, had a strong premonition of disaster about the *Titanic* and declined the position of its second engineer. The *Titanic* went down on April 14, 1912.[4]

Post a careful analysis of premonitions relating to the *Titanic* and discarding all vague forebodings, as well as after-the-event claims, ten impressive cases of precognition remained. Out of these, eight pertained to dreams. I have listed only two above.

Precognition of large-scale calamities was similarly affirmed in an incident in a little-known mining village, Aberfan in South Wales.

On October 21, 1966, a massive coal-tip slid down a mountainside and engulfed Aberfan, killing 144 people, mostly school children. The following week, in response to an appeal in a national newspaper, an English psychiatrist, Dr J. Barker, obtained a large number of reports from people who felt they had received precognitive information concerning the tragedy. After all claims were scrutinized, thirty-five cases remained that Dr Barker considered reliable. Out of these there were twenty-four cases wherein the information had been related to someone else before the landslide occurred. Dreams figured in twenty-five of the accounts.[5]

In his famous book, *An Experiment with Time*, J.W. Dunne, a military engineer, convincingly refuted the belief that precognitive dreams may be the preserve of the gifted few. Its publication in 1927 caused a sensation with its suggestion that everybody had precognitive dreams, but failed to notice them. His great interest in dreams was sparked off by a particularly impressive disaster dream. In the spring of 1902 he was encamped with the 6th Mounted Infantry in Orange Free State in South Africa. There he had had an unusually vivid dream, where he saw himself standing on an island that he had dreamt of before:

> ...*an island which was in imminent peril from a volcano. And, when I saw the vapour spouting from the ground, I gasped: 'It's the island! Good Lord, the whole thing is going to blow up!' For I had memories of reading about Krakatoa, where the sea, making its way into the heart of a volcano through a submarine crevice, flashed into steam, and blew the whole mountain to pieces. Forthwith I was seized with a frantic desire to save the four thousand (I knew the number) unsuspecting inhabitants.*

In the dream Dunne then tried to warn the French (he was sure they were French) authorities that the volcano was about to explode and that 4,000 lives were at risk.

When the next batch of newspapers arrived from Britain a few days later, the *Daily Telegraph* carried a major story on the eruption of Mount Pelée on the French island of Martinique, with the 'probable loss of over 40,000 lives'. In another column of the same paper a headline read: 'A Mountain Explodes'—exactly as Dunne had witnessed in his dream. Clearly, the dream was precognitive, but one small mysterious detail remained unexplained. It came to his attention when the next batch of papers had arrived from Britain, giving more exact figures of the actual casualties. The first reports had made one assume that the dream had neglected one zero and therefore announced the loss of lives as 4,000. The true figure of loss of lives had nothing to do with the number in his dream, or with any combination of fours and zeros. Incidentally, Dunne admits that while reading the newspaper account he had, in fact, misread 40,000 lives as 4,000, and it was only much later that he realized his mistake. Freud, we know, would have attributed this mistake to the deception of the dream work and dug into the dreamer's associational network to identify the latent content of the dream. Dunne, instead, argued otherwise: the erroneous number suggested that the dream had obtained its precognitive information not from the actual events themselves on the island of Martinique, but from the misread newspaper article. He then honestly questioned himself whether the whole thing was, what doctors call, a case of paramnesia (recall of events that had never happened)—that he had never really had any such dream, but had imagined that he had dreamt all the details given in the paper after reading the newspaper report. This distortion of memory appears to be a close cousin of retrospective falsification encountered earlier; both engender false memories.

If true, this mechanism of paramnesia would render all precognition or even all paranormal dreaming as false or deluded.

Luckily for paranormal dreaming, another of Dunne's

dreams about an unfortunate event completely squashed the paramnesia theory. The dream occurred in the autumn of 1913, wherein Dunne repeatedly saw a high railway embankment in a place that was just north of the Fifth of Forth Bridge in Scotland. The last time he witnessed this scene in his dream, a train going north had just fallen over the embankment, with several carriages lying at the bottom of a grassy slope. He gathered that the date of this occurrence was in the spring of 1914. When he awoke—and this is crucial to dispel paramnesia—he told his sister about the dream. They joked that they should warn their friends from travelling north to Scotland in the spring.

Exactly two years after the *Titanic* tragedy, on April 14, 1914, the 'Flying Scotsman', one of Britain's most famous mail trains, jumped the parapet near Burntisland Station, about fifteen miles north of the Forth Bridge, and fell onto the golf links twenty feet below.[6]

Dunne had many other clearly precognitive dreams, which led him to believe that dreams are a blend of images not only from past memories but also of future experiences. The majority of the images that have prophetic value may not be distinct and separate, but so blended and intermingled with other images that it is difficult to distinguish them as being precognitive.

Dunne cautions that when identifying future images one must not expect to come upon a complete idea or scene that may relate to a future event. This lack of connection between adjacent parts of the dream plot often results in dismissing any association between the dream and a subsequent event. At times this connection may be elusive because of a failure to take note of all the details in the dream.

Another critical point to be noted is that there has to be something odd or unusual about the image or incident for us to acknowledge it as a future correspondence. In our hunt for a future event to correspond with a specific dreamt image we would have to guard against ordinary laws of chance operating. For example, dreaming of a combination lock and then coming across one the next day perhaps may not constitute precognition.

Another reason why we fail to recognize the precognitive content in dreams, besides lack of detail, is that we are not on the lookout for it. Even though we may keep a meticulous record of our dreams we are apt to gloss the connections with waking events. Dunne posits the question to us: Why do we assume that the dream utilizes imagery only from the past and not one from the future? He cautions us to look closely for resemblances that we often miss at first glance.

Charles Dickens, much before Dunne, describes in his journal: 'I dreamed that I saw a lady in a red shawl with her back towards me... On her turning around, I found that I didn't know her and she said, "I am Miss Napier."'[7]

Dickens could not help but muse, the next morning: 'What a preposterous thing to have so very distinct a dream about nothing! And why Miss Napier? For I have never heard of any Miss Napier.' After his next public reading while he was in his retiring room, he was visited by Miss Boyle and her brother. With them was the lady in the red shawl whom they presented as Miss Napier!

Although Dickens testifies that 'these are all the circumstances exactly told', psychical researchers would be sceptical of this account and would not use this dream as evidence because it had been written only *after* his introduction to the red-shawled Miss Napier. After all, the memory of even a famous author is prone to play tricks— retrospective falsification or paramnesia. Parapsychology would require much more rigorous proof.

Dunne's personal experiments did lead to extra-sensory perception being scrutinized in research laboratories. Anecdotal accounts of paranormal dreaming have been handed down to us since antiquity, but researchers and rationalists alike have doubted their veracity on one ground or another. Validation would require controlled conditions and the elimination of all other factors that could interfere with the results. Initially, the pioneering genius of Dr Joseph B. Rhine (1895–1980), whose statistical experiments transformed psychical research into scientific parapsychology, led the way. He developed many experiments to test clairvoyance, telepathy and precognition at Duke University in the United States. His wife, Dr Louisa Rhine, worked alongside him and over twenty years collected data on 7,000 spontaneous extra-sensory episodes.[8] Her analysis showed that sixty-five per cent of these episodes occurred in dreams.

Montague Ullman and Stanley Krippner studied paranormal dreaming at the Dream Laboratory of the Maimonides Medical Center in Brooklyn, New York, set up in 1962. Their experiments were designed to weed out any factor, except paranormal dreaming, which could influence the results of their study. Their findings are summarized in their book *Dream Telepathy*.

How would you conduct an experiment to establish whether two people can communicate telepathically? Probably ask a friend to think of something and then attempt to pick up the thought. If you are successful, a critic would object that since all communication is not verbal, the message was transmitted through subtle bodily cues. The next objection could be that you know what your friend's current preoccupations are, and can thus infer his or her thoughts. Your answer must really be an educated guess and not a telepathic pick-up. It's a subtle objection, but nevertheless a valid one. At the Maimonides laboratory, Ullman and Krippner tackled these valid objections by eliminating all sensory leakage through inadvertent behavioural or subvocal clues in their experiments. Admittedly, these may appear very trivial and none of them may be significant by themselves, but taken together they could provide an avenue of subliminal perception.

The experiment involved the 'sender' and the 'receiver' and two other people. The 'receiver' was to pick up the message while sleeping in a soundproof room. Initially, the 'sender' and 'receiver' were kept in adjacent rooms, then separated to adjoining blocks, and finally kept fourteen miles apart. To eliminate any personal associations, the 'sender' was allowed no choice in the message to be communicated. A third person would choose eight coloured reproductions of paintings or sculptures and put them in envelopes. Before the 'sender' chose one envelope to communicate its contents to the 'receiver', the third person would be locked in a room for the night.

It was thus ensured that the choice of the message to be transmitted was random and that absolutely no one knew the subject matter to be communicated. When the 'receiver' entered the REM phase, a 'monitor' (the fourth person in the experiment) would alert the 'sender' by means of a buzzer. The 'sender' would then concentrate on the chosen art print, in an attempt to convey it to the 'receiver'. Towards the end of each REM period the 'receiver' would be awoken by the 'monitor' and any dream experienced recorded via an intercom. This would continue for the full night, with every recalled dream being recorded. Further, the 'monitor' too was not aware of the subject matter of the intended telepathic communication, thus eliminating the chance that he or she could by some subtle means influence the result. Could there be any further objections to the methodology used in the experiments? Apparently, yes! Maybe all the people involved in the experiment were willing believers in telepathy and therefore would be prone to read a telepathic message into the dream, thereby evaluating the dream communication to be a 'hit'. To leave no stone unturned, Ullman and Krippner sent the recorded dreams and all the eight prints to external judges who were asked to assess if there was a match between any of the prints and the dreams. They were not told which dream the 'sender' had attempted to communicate. What would you say if this procedure was followed for a series of eight nights, and thirteen such studies were carried out; that nine out of those thirteen studies showed statistically significant results? Do these experiments convince you that telepathy, dream telepathy, exists?

Of course, the 'receiver' may not have relied on telepathic sensitivity, but may have clairvoyantly 'seen' the target picture without the mediation of the 'sender's' thoughts or efforts. For this reason it may be more appropriate to call this communication extrasensory perception rather than just telepathy.

But what about precognition? Are there any experiments validating this phenomenon?

The Paranormal Dream

Two studies were done with an Englishman, Malcolm Bessent, who had a history of spontaneous precognition. In late November 1969, while staying in Brooklyn, he experienced a series of images that he felt were predictions of the future. He was urged to write them down. He sent them on December 7, 1969, to the Central Premonitions Registry (Box 482, Times Square Station, New York, NY 10036). In this he made three predictions: within four to six months' time an oil tanker would be involved in a disaster of international significance; Charles De Gaulle would die within a year; and Prime Minister Wilson would be involved in a change of government in England. All three proved to be true. In February 1970, Onassis's oil tanker, the *Arrow*, ran aground and met with disaster off the coast of Nova Scotia. Its cargo caused an oil slick that was of 'international' concern. General De Gaulle died eleven months later on November 10, 1970. And, contrary to the expectations of all political pundits and polls, Edward Heath ousted Wilson from the British government.

Impressive though this may be, Bessent accomplished a far more challenging feat. Rather than experience spontaneous precognition, he would undergo a controlled experiment and *perform*—on demand—on different nights in a long experimental series.

In the telepathy experiments done earlier at Maimonides, the choice of target was made before the dream had commenced. Now, in the precognition experiment, the target would be selected the next day, *after* the dream had been dreamt. Every care was taken that no sensory leakage took place between the dreamer or the recorder of the dream and anyone involved in choosing the target. The design of the experiment was such that the choice of the target was absolutely random. As in the case of the telepathy experiment, the assessment of whether the dream was a hit or not was left to external judges—people not involved in the experiment.

To see exactly how it worked though it may be useful to look at one night's dreams and their corresponding target. Essentially, the experiment required the selection, in the morning, of an art print which would serve as the target which the dreamer should have *already* dreamt of the previous night. Bessent's first dream was an 'impression of green and purple... Small areas of white and blue'. In the second dream of the night 'there was a large concrete building...and there was a patient from upstairs escaping... She had a white coat on, like a doctor's coat...'

The target picture was Van Gogh's *A Corridor in the Asylum*. The picture portrays a lone figure in the corridor of a mental institution that is constructed from concrete. The predominant colours are orange, green, deep blue and white.[9] Needless to say, Bessent had correctly divined what would be chosen the following morning.

The degree of success that these experiments enjoyed is almost unparalleled in the history of parapsychology. Perhaps it might just be possible to catch the echo before the sound.

In 1935, three years before his death at age 82, Freud was asked by the Hungarian writer Cornelius Tabori about his views on paranormal phenomena. Freud said, 'The transference of thoughts, the possibility of sensing the past or the future cannot be merely accidental. Some people say,' he smiled, 'that in my old age I have become credulous. No...I don't think so. Merely—all my life I have learned to accept new facts, humbly, readily.'[10]

12. Dying and Mourning

If I am asked which dreams interest people the most, my answer would surely be dreams about death. They vex us, terrify and yet fascinate us. In an effort to understand them I have divided them into three broad categories.

First, there are dreams wherein the dreamer dreams of his or her own death or sees someone close to them dying. Usually, these dreams should not be taken literally as foretelling a death. Most of them are what I term as 'psychological dreams'. Although a few of them may augur an impending death, to be precognitive they would need to possess some very strong indications, which we can't really be sure of.

In the second category of death dreams, the dreamer sees dead people come alive. These I call 'bereavement dreams' because they usually come after the death of a loved one. It has been observed time and again that the grief is accompanied by a disturbed dream life and, frequently, the deceased person lives on in these dreams.

In the third category, someone dead again appears, but the difference is that there is a tactile quality to the dream and the dreamer strongly believes that an actual contact has been made with the deceased. I simply could not sweep this category of dreams under the carpet, calling it a mere allegorical or delusional experience, because the dreamers' feelings were so strong. Since precognition is being increasingly researched nowadays, we must be able to discuss dreams of this nature too. Let us call them 'visitation' dreams.

This is a very broad categorization and an overlap may occur, leading to greater complexity in understanding a dream concerning death.

A typical dream of the first type, the psychological dream, is 'Vidya Sagar's', whom I met at a friend's house where she recounted her dream:

> *I am standing outside an operation theatre and suddenly the surgeon comes out and says to me, 'I am sorry, your husband died of a heart attack.'*
>
> *I am stunned, shocked. I don't even cry because I feel so numb.*

'I hope it doesn't signify something ominous?' Vidya asked, her voice still laced with nervousness.

'I wonder what provoked the dream. A recent bout of ill-health?' I asked, trying to eliminate the most literal rendering of the dream.

'Thank God, no,' she said.

I didn't think this dream was predicting death. In fact, dreams rarely foretell death by a direct allusion to it. If death is indicated in a dream, then it is generally couched in funerary or mourning symbols, rather than a straightforward portrayal of the person dying. These symbols aren't fixed but tend to be culture-specific, for example, Christians may dream of black clothes, while for Hindus they may be white. Also, the dream need not be couched only in *memento mori* (reminders of mortality), but can be dressed in other symbols. To the psyche, death is perhaps a transition and not an ending, thus it is seen variously as a journey, a crossing over, a barrier, a tunnel, an hourglass, the stopping of a clock, a wall (death being the great barrier), white birds, flower-filled villages, a dead tree and other such images. In the *Ramayana*, Bharat dreamt one day before his father's death that King Dashrath sank in a lake of mire, drinking oil with cupped hands. The sky was dark, the moon hung low and the trees were scorched. He then saw the King wearing a blood-red wreath speeding away on a chariot driven by an ass. However, I am not suggesting that if there are one or two symbols of mourning it predicts death. It need not. It is probably safer, and more often correct, not to interpret a dream as an indication of death, unless many elements suggest it. It is largely a question of having a 'feel' for such dreams.

A dream referring to death is often indicative of the end of something. It is a psychological death. Dreaming the death of a child may be representative of mourning the end of the dependence of the child on the parents. If the dead person is an adult, then it may signify the end of an aspect of the dreamer's psyche. If the dream is about one's own death, it usually means that big changes are ahead of us such as retirement, or a job, moving house or a close relationship. Killing someone may allude to feelings of guilt, to things that went wrong. At a subtler level, it could represent the death of feelings or the death of hope, or it could indicate the need to let go of some old, outmoded image of oneself and create room for a new one.

To return to Vidya: what could her dream signify?

Since only she could make the 'bridge', I asked her, 'What was the thing that worried you most when you woke up from the dream?'

'I would have to fend for myself all alone, given my present circumstances,' she replied promptly.

Was the dream about living alone? After some gentle probing, Vidya said that for over ten years she had lived in a large joint family that included not just her husband's parents, but also two brothers, their wives and children. They shared a common kitchen and the inevitable tensions that arise with it. Vidya had been trying to persuade her husband to move to a house of their own. He agreed to talk to his father, but she was horrified and utterly bewildered when she learnt what he had said to his father: 'I know there are tensions in the house, but I don't want to move out. Basically, it's the women's problem, not ours.'

Under the circumstances, the dream symbol of the dead husband was a potent one. The hope of a new life where her husband's loyalty would primarily be for his nuclear family instead of the joint family had 'died'. The emotions most prominent in the dream were of numbness and shock, a very close echo of Vidya's emotional state. It is fairly apparent that Vidya's dream about her husband's death was in no way foretelling it.

Does this mean there are no dreams that are warnings of death? I wish to explore my dream of many years ago, when I had started to live in the ashram.

My mother-in-law is standing in front of me, dressed in a white saree. She says, 'I just came to say goodbye.'

> *I walk with her a distance, till we reach a tunnel. I know I cannot enter the tunnel but my mother-in-law does. As she goes into the tunnel she waves, knowing I cannot follow. My last recollection of her is of a white saree-clad figure becoming more and more hazy as she disappears into the tunnel.*

Does this qualify for being a death-dream? It does not portray death but many symbols point towards it—the white saree, a tunnel (connecting the living world to that of the dead), she can enter the tunnel while I can't. She appears to be going on a journey.

Unfortunately, my mother-in-law had been diagnosed with cancer. She had undergone a radical mastectomy, but the cancer had by then spread to her lungs. She was going through a particularly difficult round of chemotherapy when I had this dream. Given this, I was inclined to treat this dream not as a symbolic one but as a death dream. Subsequent events proved that the dream-dictated indication was correct. My mother-in-law succumbed three months later to cancer, which had by then spread to her brain.

Since ancient times, people all over the globe have wondered which dream should be treated as true and which as false. Experience, presumably, taught them that their methods of classification could identify some dreams that came true and others that did not. Refinements were, of course, introduced: the circumstance of the dreamer was also considered in addition to the content of the dream. The same dream dreamt by two people with dissimilar life situations could have entirely different meanings. The

Matsya Purana lists auspicious dreams, which promise wealth, but for a sick person they foretell a quick cure. The time when a dream was dreamt would also influence whether it came true or not.

My dream is not necessarily a prognostication, it can also be validly interpreted as a psychological dream. It came at a stage when I was finding it very difficult to relinquish my city ways for the rural life that we were now leading at my Teacher's hermitage. It could be alluding to the death of an old way of life. My mother-in-law could represent another part of me that was moving ahead into a changed lifestyle. Since the farming life was unfamiliar to me, the dream symbolized it as an area of darkness—a tunnel. It could have been cautioning me to leave my city persona (symbolized by 'me' in the dream) behind in order to cope with the changed circumstances.

~

Death dreams that do not depict someone dying but bring alive a dead person in a strange reversal of reality can fascinate as also torment us deeply; we are never sure whether we are actually communicating with the departed or not.

Many times, the departed come in our dreams to say goodbye. Mine could also be seen as one such. A mother, aware that her end was imminent, had wished to bid farewell to her son. She had 'come', but not finding her son open to such communication, she did the next best thing—saying goodbye to his wife. Since she had not actually died when the dream had come it does not qualify for the dead coming alive in a dream. My next example fits the bill much better.

A balding, bespectacled man in his late fifties approached me in the library where I write, and whispered, 'May I talk to you about something?'

The man gravely looked down at the floor, recollecting his thoughts, 'My dead father has come twice to me in the last week.'

Left unsaid was that he had *dreamt* of his deceased father. His dream must have been too real for him to simply ignore, and yet his rational side didn't know how to understand it.

'And what does he say in the dream?'

'That's the problem!' the man exclaimed. 'He just stands at the foot of my bed and keeps on looking at me, as though he wants to say something.'

A part of him believed he had seen his father's ghost and the other part was afraid that he might be hallucinating. My suggestion that it was a normal bereavement dream helped him to relax a little.

'How long ago did your father…?'

'Three weeks. He died in his sleep. Our family physician said it was a silent heart attack.'

'What do you think he wants to say to you?'

'Goodbye. We could not manage that with his sudden departure. We had dinner together the previous night and the next morning he had gone,' the man said softly.

Many of the people I met reported similar dreams of dead parents, spouses, siblings, uncles, aunts and friends. Perhaps their psyche is still dealing with the loss. Research has shown that after the death of a significant person in our life our dreams go through various phases, depending upon the stage of mourning, the recentness of the loss and the nature of the death. Investigators describe at least three phases of mourning.[1]

Initially, there is *numbness*, which is characterized by shock or denial of the death, and the feeling that the events are unreal. Usually, immediately after the death, a typical class of dreams are experienced, in which the deceased is suffering the same symptoms that caused the death. Equally common are dreams that suggest the reverse, the deceased is alive and well again, and the dreamer is surprised to see him or her and the death is explained away as a mistake.

I did wonder what the purpose was of these dreams; they seem to intensify the sense of loss. That is, till a woman told me that she looks forward to sleep, in case she dreams of her dead husband! Perhaps the psyche needs to gradually digest the finality of the separation.

After the period of numbness somewhat wears off, there may follow a phase in which there is emotional chaos. There can be feelings of regret, grief, anger or guilt. The survivor feels distanced from life; many questions arise, and they grope for answers. There can be restlessness stemming from the need to somehow know where the deceased has gone. My library acquaintance's dream may have come at the end of such a phase. The need for 'goodbye' may signify the end of his confusion and the need to return to everyday life.

In the last phase, the survivor slowly learns to cope with the changed environment, and at the same time treasures memories of the departed. I must add that this does not mean that everyone's grief registers in such clear-cut stages; often it oscillates between them.

Dr 'Toshi Talwar's' husband died of an ulcerated intestine, largely due to errors made by the doctors operating on him. She had watched him die in considerable pain, leaving her, in her late twenties, with their four-year-old daughter. She had to deal with the anger she felt towards the doctors who had operated on him. Added to this was her own sense of helplessness in being unable to save her husband despite being a doctor. Six months later, on the eve of her birthday, she saw her husband in a dream: 'It was the same smile, the same look that he had in life, and he said to me, "You think I could forget your birthday?" Unlike my last memory of him, when pain had ravaged his face, in my dream he looked younger, without a trace of pain. In fact, much to my surprise, he looked totally at peace. He hugged me and then said goodbye. I was so happy to see him that I awoke with tears in my eyes.'

Her eyes still held the wonder of that encounter even though she was much older now. 'The incident did not end with the dream. Not only did he remember my birthday, he also sent me a gift!'

By a very curious coincidence the cheque for her husband's life insurance policy arrived the next day—on her birthday. For Dr Talwar, it was immensely reassuring: her husband had not deserted her.

The reassurance can also come in the form of another kind of gift. William Blake, who was greatly grieved on his brother's death, dreamt that Robert appeared and taught him an innovative method of engraving.[2] Blake did try out his brother's suggestions and found they were ideal for inexpensively engraving his illustrations.

In some instances the departed can also criticize the living. The British writer Virginia Woolf had an ambivalent relationship with her father, both admiring him and resenting him for his treatment of her sister. Four years after his death, she dreamt of showing him the manuscript of a novel she had begun to write. He read her work, snorted, and dropped it onto a table. She awoke, melancholic and discouraged.[3]

~

We now come to the third type of death dream, the controversial visitation dream. But why do the dead appear to us in dreams? After all, one phase of human existence is over, death has cast its veil, and the edict should not be tampered with by backward glances. After hearing the experience of the Sikands, I can only say—it happens.

At some point or the other, each of us has to face our own mortality and enquire whether our end is merely in the dissolution of the body, or whether we will survive its death.

Colonel Surinder Sikand's mother suffered a coronary thrombosis and lapsed into a coma at the age of fifty-two. On the tenth night of her coma, he dreamt:

> *Strangely, I find my mother sitting on my bed and she says, 'I'm going, Surinder. My time is up. But I am concerned about your father. Please look after him after I am gone.'*

Surinder Sikand awoke, switched on the light, and, rousing his sleeping wife Sarla, pronounced, 'Mother is no more.'

Half an hour later the phone rang to confirm the news of his mother's passing.

Surinder reminisced: 'I think she was concerned how my father would handle life without her. They were very close to one another.'

'You believe she came to tell you to look after him,' I ventured.

'What else could it be?'

Silence filled the room as we realized we were treading on unknown ground; a terrain where personal experience and belief is all the proof there is to map the way.

'Did you somehow know she would never come out of the coma, so that the dream was more of a confirmation than a visitation?'

'Yes, we knew her condition was critical. But I knew that on the previous night too. Why didn't I have the dream one night earlier? Was it not rather coincidental that I dreamt about her more or less at the exact time of her death? Her "coming" and then my father immediately confirming her death over the phone is uncanny.'

Besides Colonel Sikand's own conviction, I also knew that his dream did not fit into any of the categories of bereavement dreams. Initially, it seemed to be a straightforward case of a 'saying-goodbye' dream, except that he did not know his mother was dead, so the question of bereavement did not arise. We are not in the same dilemma as with my dream of my mother-in-law entering a tunnel. That was precognitive and not a visitation as she was alive at the time of the dream. Here, the dream and his mother's demise were roughly concurrent; precognition may not be that appropriate an explanation. Perhaps telepathy may be a more plausible one. But does that make it more rational?

However, if we grudgingly concede to visitations, then we are seized with a further difficulty: Who is it that visits? The person without the body, but complete with personality traits and memories, as was apparent in this case? Do the dead live on as more or less the same people we knew them to be?

This became even more apparent when Surinder's mother made another visit soon after. 'His mother *came* one and a half months later to Mr Goel,' Surinder's wife Sarla informed me.

'Who is Mr Goel?' I asked.

'He was the accountant at the Lady Linlithgow Tuberculosis Centre, in New Delhi, which my father-in-law had headed.' He dreamt that Surinder's mother told him:

In the large steel trunk, which has all the blankets and quilts, under the green quilt right at the bottom, there are a thousand rupees which I had saved. Could you inform Dr Sikand about this money as I had never told him or anyone else about it?

Mr Goel mentioned the dream to Dr Sikand. The old man became emotional and immediately went to the store adjacent to the kitchen to open the steel trunk. Narinder, his younger son, seeing that his father was getting rather upset, tried to distract him by saying, 'Daddy, you know that mother was not the kind of person who could save money. She enjoyed spending it, and tucking a thousand rupees under some quilts seems not only out of character for her, but impossible.'

Dr Sikand was not to be stopped; he opened the

trunk and started hunting for the money. Barely had he gone through the top three or four layers when Narinder intervened: 'There is nothing here. You believe a mere dream! Why are we upsetting ourselves by going through with this?'

Narinder managed to persuade his father to leave the storeroom. None of them really believed Mr Goel's dream, except Dr Sikand. It seemed that the matter had ended. Evidently not, for old Dr Sikand was biding his time, waiting for Narinder to leave town. He then insisted on taking Sarla back to the storeroom and to the large trunk.

Sarla felt a little uncomfortable at his insistence, yet she felt compassion for him—for his search for anything connected with his wife.

'I still remember the moment I opened the trunk,' Sarla recalled, 'how the smell of dried Neem leaves hit me. Oddly enough a strange expectancy filled the room as I began lifting the quilts out of the trunk, to reach the lower layers. When I neared the bottom my father-in-law gently placed his hand on my elbow and said, "Please, let me check."

'Daddyji paused when he uncovered the last layer to reveal a green velvet quilt. He looked at me and said, "Exactly as she said!" I stood there amazed. Mr Goel couldn't have known this! Daddyji lifted the quilt first from one side, then from the other. Sure enough there were a wad of currency notes of all denominations. Very slowly he counted it. It was a thousand rupees!

'What can I say except that for more than a long moment we both stood there, in utter silence? None of us knew anything about the money. Had my dead mother-in-law actually come to Mr Goel? Hadn't she conveyed a straightforward message?'

It seemed as if Sarla Sikand's last remark was aimed at my doubts that began with 'Could it be that...' I must confess that most of my objections were silenced. My only question was, 'I wonder why she *came* to Mr Goel, and not to a family member?'

'I don't know. Except that she often relied on Mr Goel for small errands like getting a plumber, buying train or movie tickets, paying bills...'

'As in life so in death,' I said.

'What do you mean?'

'Your mother-in-law depended on Mr Goel for some of the nitty-gritty details of everyday life. Probably this money fell under the same category.'

The 'message' of Mr Goel's dream can hardly be thought of as symbolic. It would have been a symbolic dream if the money had not been found. For the Sikands, the reality of hard currency notes was a testimony of her 'visit'.

It is said that the memory of anything we see or hear, even subliminally, is stored in our brain. The theory of cryptoamnesia suggests that the number of flagstones that paved the walk I took with my mother at the age of six still resides somewhere within my mind. Nothing is ever forgotten. Could dreams be one mode of spontaneous access to this store? In Mr Goel's case there were no means by which he could have known that Mrs Sikand had hidden the money in the trunk. So where did his dream access this information?

It may be pointed out that this is not an isolated

dream; there are many other such accounts. Perhaps the earliest reference to a visitation dream is from the *Iliad*: the spirit of the slain Patroclus appears before Achilles and demands burial.[4]

Perhaps we wouldn't find visitation dreams such a challenge to our rationality if we didn't see death in such harsh and final terms. Some cultures see death as a journey whose final goal is the recovery of our essential self.

In some traditions dreaming of death was seen as a good sign, thought of as predicting news of birth. The Tibetans cast an astrological chart for the moment of death to 'see' what sort of life will befall the deceased in the future. Of course, these conclusions can never be proven but they still persist in their culture. The Egyptians believed dreams of coffins represented rebirth, like that of Osiris after his cut body had been entombed in a casket and his resurrection was seen as proof of life eternal. In that sense death dreams may paradoxically be closely linked to renewal. The *psychological*-death dream represents another life, a new road, a fresh start. Our bereavement dreams may signify the effort towards renewal. Dreaming of one's own death could be at a fundamental level a less fearful dress rehearsal to help confront our mortality as though we are leaving one room to go to another. A journey without an end but which has many seasons. Those who have journeyed on seem to remain fundamentally the same people we knew and loved. Whatever we were to one another, we still are. When occasionally they glance back to 'visit', there seems an absolute and unbroken continuity of association.

This unbroken continuity between life and death was

encountered by British psychoanalyst Dr Jay Dunn too. Dunn was attending a hospitalized patient, 'Margot', an elderly woman suffering the final stages of a terminal ailment. She reported to her doctor a dream whose metaphorical image is as simple as it is profound.[5]

She sees a candle lit on the window sill of the hospital room and finds that the candle suddenly goes out. Fear and anxiety ensue as the darkness envelops her. Suddenly, the candle lights on the other side of the window and she awakens.

That same day Margot died, and in Dr Dunn's words, completely at peace.

13. Awake and Dreaming— The Lucid Dream

I dreamed that I was walking by the water on the shore. It was morning; the sky a light blue; the foam-flecked waves were greenish in the sunshine. I forget just how it happened, but something told me that I was dreaming... I decided to prolong the dream and continued my walk, the scenery now appearing extraordinarily vivid and clear. Very soon my body began to draw me back. I experienced dual consciousness: I could feel myself lying in bed and walking by the sea at one and the same time. Moreover, I could dimly see the objects of my bedroom, as well as the dream scenery. I willed myself to continue dreaming. A battle ensued; now my bedroom became clearly visible and the shore-scene dim; then my bedroom would become indistinct and the shore-scene brighter. My will triumphed. I lost the sense of dual consciousness. My bedroom faded altogether from my vision, and I was out on the shore feeling indescribably free and elated.[1]

This dream is unusual because the dreamer is on the verge of waking up but attempts to snatch a few more moments of sleep, to walk along the shore canopied by a light blue sky. In fact, the dream begins by informing the dreamer that morning has come and that maybe it is time to wake up. There is, however, another unusual feature: the dreamer is not going linearly from one state to the other, from sleep to waking, but instead, experiences dual consciousness—is asleep and also awake, for he or she can dimly see the objects of the bedroom as well as the scenery along the sea shore. Then, for a while, the dream state dominates and the shore-scene becomes clearly visible and the bedroom dims. This reverses as the battle rages within and changes direction. The dreamer can also exercise choice—to walk along the shore—a feature we know is totally absent in normal dreams.

Is the difference between this dream and others the ability to choose? A regular dream is like a movie being screened and you are lost to yourself, completely enraptured. In the dream above, however, the dreamer is a participant and can affect the course of the movie. This is in contrast with 'normal' dreams, since the dreamer is aware that he or she is dreaming. This type of dream, with its quality of dual awareness, is called a 'lucid' dream. The term was coined by Frederik van Eeden who used the word 'lucid' to indicate mental clarity while dreaming. The great contradiction of lucid dreaming is that the private, unconscious world of normal dreaming inexplicably melts into a state where you are both awake (conscious) and asleep simultaneously.

The dream narrated above highlights some typical elements of lucid dreams. As we notice, the dreamer is not completely immersed in the dream, and is in fact aware of dreaming. Normal memory is available during the dream: *'my body began to draw me back'*; *'my bedroom became clearly visible'*. After becoming lucid, the dream becomes very vivid; the attainment of lucidity helps the dreamer experience the dream more intensely. Lastly, after a little vacillation, the dreamer takes control of the experience, exercising the choice to continue the dream-walk along the shore, rather than wake up. To summarize the features of lucid dreaming: the dreamer can access normal memory by stepping back from the dream, over which there is volitional control, and which is characterized by greater vividness, though all these elements may not necessarily be present.

Here's another example:

I am going down a flight of stairs and reach a landing. I can either turn left or go right. Both are staircases that lead down. I automatically turn right and descend a steep flight of stairs which seem never to end. The engulfing darkness frightens me. I suddenly realize I am dreaming. I decide to go back and explore the turn to the left. The dream is continuing without my falling asleep again. I seem to know what is happening to me. Am I awake or asleep? I am back at the landing and turn to the left. My fear gives way to a growing excitement. I realize this is the Imambara in Lucknow. I know I am on the right track; the staircase is familiar. Then I wake up.

We see, once again, in this dream, that waking memory is available to the dreamer, thought can be directed, and the dreamer can reason while continuing to dream. When awake, we voluntarily decide on our course of action—whether to turn left or right, or talk to a stranger or not. This volitional control was also present within this dream. It is a lucid dream.

Usually, when inexperienced dreamers realize that they are dreaming, the sudden perception of 'lucidity' can jolt them into waking up and the dream experience then ends. That does not happen here, even though the dreamer wonders if he is 'awake or asleep', the dream continues without a break. In fact, in the earliest stage of lucidity the dreamer may experience volitional control over the course of the dream in a variety of ways. Lucidity can occur with the dreamer unable to clearly ascertain whether he or she is awake or dreaming, or even when there is a false awakening—the dreamer awakes within the dream, but is left with the feeling that he or she has awoken from sleep.

Lucidity is often triggered when the dreamer finds something odd (bizarre) within the dream and wonders whether it is real, like the fright in the above dream. This thought could lead to the realization that 'If this isn't real then I must be dreaming', and the dreamer becomes lucid. However, some episodes of lucidity can be spontaneously triggered.[2]

The awakeness in a lucid dream, though it shares some aspects with our habitual waking experience, is of a different order. Perhaps this awakeness is neither derived purely from waking cognition, nor is it a refinement of it.

Despite many individual accounts of lucid dreaming, claims about their validity have been strongly discounted on philosophical grounds: How can a person be conscious while dreaming? These lucid dreams are explained away as brief or partial arousals—micro-awakenings. The dreamer may have, it is argued, awoken for a fraction of a second and the memory of that micro-awakening had lingered through the dream, leaving an impression of being awake during the course of the dream. Or, alternately, there was a false awakening, in which the dreamer woke up as part of the dream but felt he had awoken from sleep.

We cannot say what had actually transpired in the dream about the Imambara, whether the dreamer had become conscious while sleeping, or there had been a micro-awakening, or a false awakening, as the dreamer states *'the dream is continuing without my falling asleep again'*.

Seductive though these objections are, we now have concrete proof that this is not the mechanism of a lucid dream. Research laboratories on both sides of the Atlantic have conclusively settled the debate on the reality of lucid dreams. The sleep patterns of dreamers experiencing lucidity while dreaming were closely monitored in a laboratory. Since human physiology registers the three states of waking, sleeping and dreaming differently, researchers can immediately detect the onset of a dream and also whether the dreamer has momentarily awoken before wafting back into the dream. Laboratory research belied the arousal mechanism, but the truly impressive aspect of these studies was not simply the confirmation of lucid dreams, but the fact that the researchers devised a way by which the dreamer could communicate with them while simultaneously continuing to experience a dream! How could there be communication between someone awake and someone asleep? We are not alluding to hearing someone talk while asleep. Researchers did manage to find a way past this dilemma.

Since the muscular system is inert during a dream, the only signal for the onset of lucidity could be exaggerated eye movements. During ordinary dreaming the eye movements are usually involuntary. However, if, while dreaming, a person made specific, pre-arranged ocular movements, for example moving the eyes left to right three times and then stopped, it would convincingly demonstrate that the person was 'lucid', and the laboratory equipment would testify that he or she was asleep and experiencing a dream. Subjectivity during this experiment was eliminated. EOG (electrooculogram) pen tracings were used to pick up the eye movements to constitute an objective record of the onset of lucidity.

The incontestable hold of waking experience on reality was questioned in the West in 1985, when lucid dreaming was irrefutably demonstrated in the laboratory. It rudely shattered the dichotomy between the irrationality of the dream world and the sanity of the waking world. All the distinctions between the subjective world of dreaming and the objective world of waking, between lonely or shared, private or public, involuntary or conscious were dissolved. If dreaming shares with waking experience common capacities and abilities—like the ability to reflect and make choices—then don't the boundaries between waking and sleeping, conscious and unconscious or real and imaginary break down? This questioning is necessitated by the capability of lucid dreamers to be simultaneously awake and asleep.

The misconception that dreams are purely mental

activity and have no effect on the body was dispelled by lucid dreamers. Experiments conducted by Stephen LaBerge at the Stanford University Sleep Research laboratories addressed a larger range of issues that helped understand the dream state as well as explore its connections with waking reality.

In these carefully controlled experiments, it was demonstrated that if the breath was held, or breathing was rapid, in the dream, then corresponding changes were initiated in the sleeper's actual pattern of breathing.[3]

It is known that the two hemispheres of the brain are used for differing everyday activities: the left hemisphere shows increased activity during language use and analytical thinking, while the right shows increased activity during spatial tasks and holistic thinking. Differing activities like counting and singing were performed by people while awake and their cerebral hemispherical activity noted. Would similar results hold during REM dreaming? Indeed, the same patterns of selective activation while singing and counting were observed during dreaming as they were during wakefulness.[4]

A very interesting experiment concerning the lapse of time during the dream state was carried out. The dreamer was asked to count from 1 to 10 in order to measure the lapse of ten seconds of time while dreaming. The lucid dreamer would signal the commencement and end of a session of counting to researchers, who would measure the time taken with a stopwatch. It took the dreamer thirteen seconds (by the stopwatch) to count from one to ten. This would seem to indicate that the passage of time is slower in dreams than in the waking world. However, when the same dreamer was asked to count up to ten while awake, it still measured thirteen seconds by the stopwatch![5] This showed that the lapse of time while dreaming is for all practical purposes the same as while awake!

Then there was another question: Was sexual activity in lucid dreams accompanied by physiological changes similar to those that take place during waking sexual activity? A pilot study with two lucid dreamers reported sexual arousal and orgasm in lucid dreams and revealed patterns of physiological activity during dream-sex that closely resembled corresponding experiences in a waking state, except the rise in heart rate.[6]

What these experiments proved was that lucid dreams seem to break all rules that we have framed for reality. If dream-sex is akin to the experience of sex while awake, if the lapse of time in dreams and waking life is the same, if counting and singing in dreams are like 'real' singing and counting, then these experiments provide evidence that dreaming of doing something is closer to actually doing it than imagining it. If dream reality produces the same physiological changes that a similar event in waking life does, then why should we assume that one set of experiences—the waking ones—are 'real' and the other—the dream experiences—are unreal?

The quality of vividness in a lucid dream is such that it seems to verge on full wakefulness. Yet the lucid dream is distinct from most of our waking experiences and it also appears to be different from our normal dream experience. Lucid dreams refuse to be billeted into the traditional definition of dreaming.

The quality of 'lucidity' can and does vary greatly in

the various cases of lucid dreams reported or studied. The hallmark of 'normal' dreams is that the dreamer does not have the ability to reflect like we do when we are awake. However, when lucid, the dreamer does have this self-referential ability. It may well be that even our everyday dreams are part of a continuum in which there are gradations of self-reference or self-reflection. At one end of this continuum we may find a complete absence of self-reflection in dreams. In other dreams there may be an incremental increase in self-awareness, where the dreamer is dimly aware that he or she is dreaming and is conscious in patches of what is happening in the dream. This awareness will be seen to advance in some other dreams, till a stage is reached in which the dreamer has a sustained awareness of what is actually happening—specifically that he or she is asleep in bed and dreaming.

At the lowest level of this continuum, the dreamer is not present in the dream and the dream involves unknown people and unfamiliar objects. For example: *The police were chasing a man down an alley.* The dreamer is not a part of the dream and hence there is no self-reference in the dream. Self-reference in dreams moves a step upwards when the dreamer is a part of the dream, and the dreamer's attention is completely soaked in the action within the dream: *The police were chasing me; I was cornered in an alley with no chance of escape.* These are our normal dreams. One level higher on the scale and the dreamer is able to think over an idea and reflect upon the action in the dream or communicate with someone else. For example: *I watched the police chase a man down my alley and wondered if he was a terrorist. My neighbour tells me: This is a fake encounter, a set-up.* An even higher stage is attained when the dreamer has multiple levels of awareness, and notices oddities while dreaming. For example: *As I was running from the police, I wondered whether they would believe me if I surrendered and told them I was innocent. I then noticed that there were no doors opening into the alley, only windows, and all of them were barred. My only chance of escape was to scale the wall.* Here, the dreamer, while participating in the dream action, also reflects on intentions, monitors progress and ponders about behaviour modification. One more step and the dreamer, from simultaneously participating and reflecting within the dream, may consciously deliberate whether he or she is dreaming: *The police were chasing me and I saw my father standing at each doorway in the alley looking disgustedly at me. I found this very odd—how could my father be in so many places at the same time? I then realized that I was dreaming and all the anxiety of the police chasing me disappeared. I turned and faced the police and they all smiled at me.* The dreamer has become lucid by noticing the oddity in the dream.

Is lucidity then an aberration of the dreaming process, a dream gone bizarre? Is the dreaming process going against its own grain? Because the dreaming brain exhibits very different characteristics from the sleeping brain, dreams have been called paradoxical sleep. Similarly, lucidity has been viewed as paradoxical dreaming because it is very different from ordinary dreaming—it involves dual consciousness. Perhaps this is why lucid dreams constitute a challenge to our worldview.

In fact, the most important question that lucidity raises pertains actually to the waking state. When lucid we are able to realize that we are dreaming while dreaming. Do we ever notice or question whether we are awake while we are awake? Furthermore, do we enquire what in fact it means to be 'awake'? Lucid dreams force us to revise our understanding of the awake–asleep boundary.[7] Perhaps 'awakeness' is a form of consciousness that is not always chained to the waking state, just like being asleep is not the fundamental prerequisite for dreaming.

Perhaps this elasticity of the dreaming mind can stretch far beyond the by now familiar dimensions of dreaming and reveal states of consciousness whose outer form is glimpsed in traditional religions and their practices. History bears out that dreams have served as an important vehicle for religious inspiration. In fact, we find that some form of dream imagery is embedded in the beginning of most if not all major religions of the world.

In Christianity many of the events surrounding the birth and early life of Christ were announced by dreams. Joseph was told the source of Mary's pregnancy in a dream and was instructed to name the child Jesus. In later dreams Joseph was warned that he should flee to Egypt with Mary and the child to avoid Herod's diktat of killing all male infants. Judaism also places a lot of emphasis on dreams. In the sixty-three volumes of the Talmud there are 217 references to dreams attributed to many different sages and scholars.[8]

Even a cursory look at Buddhist literature reveals that the Buddha's mother, Queen Maya, dreamt in 544 BCE of the future Buddha's birth. Also, 'five of the Buddha's dreams, along with dreams of his father, King [S]udhodana, and his wife, Gopa, appear in the Pali scriptures and describe his future vocation as a wandering monk'.[9] Similarly in Islam, Prophet Muhammad (570–632 CE) received his divine mission in a dream. In fact, much of the Koran was revealed in his dreams over a period of several years. Every morning he would share his dreams with his followers, as well as ask them for their dreams and offer interpretations.[10] It was during his lifetime that dream interpretation became a science called *Ilm al-tabir*.[11]

At this point, the following objection could be raised: If these religious dreams simply announce future circumstances like the paranormal dream, why do we need to identify a different dimension of dreaming? The difference between them is that ordinary dreams that offer prognostication are primarily concerned with mundane events and mostly affect the dreamer. Dreams of religious prophecy can sometimes affect an entire race, like the dreams announcing the birth of Gautama Buddha and Jesus Christ. Such visions act as the eyes of the race, transcending personal biographies to announce the intersection of the transpersonal with the mundane. Clearly, there is a need for a different dimension or paradigm of dreaming that takes into account religious dreams. Nor should it be confused with the 'god-sent' dream of antiquity. Further, the religious dream or vision is not limited only to the announcements of the coming of world saviours. The Muslim philosopher Ibn Arabi (1164–1240) argued that there exists a type of dream that is sourced directly from the 'Universal Soul' or the 'Guarded Table'. 'In such a dream man's (rational) soul perceives the archetypal ideas contained in the Universal Soul… Imagination does not enter into it, and the "inward eye" reproduces the exact reflection of the impression received... They are the direct vision of Reality, of Universal Truth.'[12] This knowledge, it was argued, was possible only in a state of suspension from the outer senses, which normally occurs during sleep or in deep contemplation. This is the second type of religious dream, the mystical dream. It penetrates beyond material things to that immaterial Reality that some call the Absolute and most theologians call God.

One of the great Christian theologians and contemplatives, Denis the Carthusian (1402–1471), succinctly clarifies the distinction between the two types of religious dreams: 'The first kind are to be concealed, the second declared. The first are truly mystic, the second prophetic...'[13] The mystical dream has not been written about as openly or as frequently as the religious prophetic dream.

The mystical dream has many dimensions. At its best it is another view of reality different from our waking one. To appreciate this, our classification of waking and dreaming may need to be questioned. The Hindu-Buddhist asks why we are confusing dreaming, which is actually a state of consciousness, with the state of the body—waking or sleeping. Normally, we assume that the dream is a state connected to sleep wherein we enter a private, imaginary world in which external reality does not intrude, and herein we relinquish the voluntary direction of attention. If this defines the dream then don't all these characteristics apply to our daydreams, as also to the reverie, the trance and the hypnotic state? In all these the body is in the waking state while our consciousness is more akin to the dream state. Wouldn't it be better to think of dreaming as a state of consciousness rather than limit it to the condition of the body? Herein lies the significance of lucid dreaming, which demonstrably breaks the connection of dream consciousness with a supine body. While asleep the lucid dreamer can voluntarily direct attention and is aware of where he or she is. In short, by conventional definitions, he or she is awake and asleep simultaneously.

Lucid dreaming has been the prerogative of religious/mystical schools because it points to another state of consciousness. Most religious texts also exhort the novice to 'awake', 'watch', 'sleep not' and so on. Perhaps the realization of this state of awakeness is what transcendental or mystical dreaming also strives towards.

Psychological studies affirm the link between lucidity and meditation. It is estimated that nearly six out of ten people experience a lucid dream once in their life. Maybe only two people out of them have a lucid dream once a month. However, if the sample interviewed comprises people who practise meditation, then the average goes up to once a week. Other studies confirm that experienced meditators have significantly more lucid dreams than non-meditating dreamers. It has also been shown that the longer a person has been engaged in meditative practice (an average of five years), more frequent are the reports of lucid and control dreams—to the point where some subjects could not tell whether they were having a lucid dream or whether they had awakened and were spontaneously meditating. Still other studies have borne out that the physiological state during lucid dreaming may be closely related to changes in EEG results and other markers associated with meditation. These findings have raised the issue of similarities and parallels between what lucid dreaming and meditational states can achieve, especially in the attempt to harness consciousness towards higher levels of awareness.

Perhaps the onset of lucid dreaming initiates a process in which an actual separation takes place between a part of the self that consciously reflects that it is dreaming and another part that participates or is involved in the dream itself. In other words, there is a focus of awareness separate from the activity in the dream—the dreamer shifts from being only a participant in the dream to also becoming its observer. This can evolve to a point where the action in the dream no longer remains the dominant focus; it does not grip the dreamer such that he or she stays identified with it. With this further separation the person climbs to the upper reaches of lucidity—by staying in sheer observation. Unlike the typical lucid state in which the waking-state self can function from within the dream, an unbounded Self now silently observes from outside the dream state.[14]

The various meditational schools remind the novice that lucidity is not merely the process of self-reflection that we sometimes indulge in during our waking hours—the process by which we become aware of our thoughts, feelings or behaviour. This too involves a division between our observing self and a participating self. However, the self-as-observer is not the same as the witnessing consciousness of the mystic or the *sakshi chaitanya* of the Hindus. In self-reflection the observer evaluates (judges) and desires to alter the participant. That is, the observer is identified with the participant. Here the division that is usually effected is between what we like in ourselves or what we imagine is strong within us and that which we do not like or consider to be weak within us.[15] This is not the division that meditational schools value. What they call witnessing consciousness is an entirely different state of awareness that goes beyond self-reflection. It may observe the participating self, but it has no investment in it. Unlike self-reflection, it witnesses without involvement, without any trace of fear or desire—good or bad. Usually in life this witnessing awareness is passive and seldom brought to the forefront of consciousness; it is not the self which thinks, acts and reflects.

In dreaming, this is the point of departure between the mundane and religious/mystical schools. The former believes the actual state of lucidity is the ultimate destination—the thraldom of clarity and of freedom to direct their effort towards creating new and different forms of experience within the dream. I have never been on a luxury liner, so let me have the thrill of a cruise on an ocean-going luxury yacht. More often than not all that this thirst for novelty will aim to do is to fulfil ungratified desires.

The mystic's approach, on the other hand, is directed towards transcending the dream state rather than simply subjugating it to fulfil desires through it. The aspirant on the mystical path is not interested merely in a balance between observation and involvement, but aims to attain a state of total withdrawal from participation in the dream such that it leads to a condition of mindfulness.

The mystical/religious schools take a turn at the fork in the road that traverses a totally different terrain. For the religious novice the emergence of the simplest form

The Lucid Dream

of lucidness may become a bridge to this witnessing consciousness. Since this observational state is initially fragile and can easily be shattered, the first step then is to stabilize lucidity—make it mindful—so that it does not lapse back into the unawareness of ordinary dreaming. The lucid state, and especially the dual awareness of being the participant and the observer, can be further developed by withdrawing the attention from the participant and resting it completely within the calmness of the observer. And this is to be effected with no deliberate intervention in dream content. In this instance, absolutely no feelings and ideas whatsoever stand between the observer and the events of the dream. The action in the dream goes on 'out there' but the observer chooses not to pay attention to it, identifying instead completely with the awareness that observes the dream. A tranquil observation resting in itself. If there is any vested interest (attachments and preferences) in any aspect of the dream, then the observational mode is abandoned and the attention is sucked back into participation in the dream.

Lest it be believed that these are but rarefied states of consciousness, mere metaphysical speculations, let us look at scientific studies that confirm some of these transformations of consciousness. North American researchers like Harry Hunt, Jayne Gackenbach and Charles Alexander (among many others) have begun to identify and detail in their experimental subjects this initial separation of awareness from the action in the dream. Gackenbach conducted a study with sixty-six advanced meditators (people who had been meditating for more than twenty years) and was able to identify a state of consciousness that she calls 'witnessing dreaming'. In contrast to lucid dreaming, she defines witnessing dreaming as an experience of quiet, peaceful inner awareness or wakefulness, completely separate from the dream. She had to use a specialized group for the study because these states under investigation are so subtle that college students would not have been able to recognize or identify them.[16] The study yielded fifty-five lucid dream descriptions and forty-one witnessing dreaming descriptions. 'Most revealing of these categories was the one on feelings of separateness. In lucid dreaming only 7 percent of the cases were those in which people reported feeling separateness. In the witnessing dream experience, 73 percent of the cases spontaneously reported in their dream description that the dream went on, but they were separate from it.'[17]

Gackenbach aptly describes these states through the experiences of a mathematics professor who had practised transcendental meditation for twenty years. 'In the beginning, this person talked about lucid dreams he had in which the actor was dominant. Here the role of the observer is to recognize that the self is dreaming, but despite this recognition, the feeling still exists that the dream is out there and the self is in here. When you are in the dream, the dream still feels real.

'As you become more familiar with lucidity it may occur to you that you can manipulate, change or control the dream. In a second stage it occurred to this dreamer that what is "out there" is actually in some sense "in here". The dreamer may actively engage [in] the dream events or control and manipulate them.

'In a third stage his dreams became short. He described them as being like thoughts that arose, which he took note of and then let go.'[18]

'"The action of the dream," he says, "is not dominant. It does not grip you so that you are [not] identified with it as opposed to the first step in which the focus was more on the active [participation]. In this case it's just a state of inner awareness that's really dominant. Awareness is there very strongly. The dream is a little dust flying about so to speak."

'[In a fourth stage he discovered that] an "inner wakefulness" dominates. "You don't have dreams or in any case you don't remember having dreams." He was not absorbed in the dreams but in witnessing.'[19] Gackenbach goes on to conclude that in witnessing dreaming the person can manipulate the dream, but simply does not desire to do so. Whatever the content of the dream, the person feels an inner tranquillity that keeps him or her removed from the dream. At times the dreamer does get snared again in the events of the dream, but the background of a peaceful inner awareness remains. Some subjects were also able to retain this witnessing state during dreamless sleep. They reported a silent state of inner wakefulness with no object of thought or perception. Gackenbach calls this state 'witnessing deep-sleep', in which there is a feeling of infinite expansion and bliss and nothing else.

This, then, seems to be a totally different role of the dream. It is no longer merely a source of prophecy, nor is it yoked to the material weight of the day world. Here dreams are the vehicles of salvational practices, capable of insights that are not borrowed from the rational waking world, but insights that can alter forever the way mundane reality is perceived. The dream is not a metaphor for the waking self and its concerns; instead, it is viewed as the training ground for the transformation of consciousness.

In the next chapter I discuss my dreams, not as a mirror of the personality but as a gateway to transcendence.

14. Self-Enquiry and Dreams: Dreaming in a Himalayan Monastery[1]

Dreams, according to Ashishda, are also a way of self-enquiry in the disciple's journey. They are the *switch-points* that allow a two-way view of the outer and inner realms. On this journey, different types of dreams occur that increasingly step away from the personal and allow glimpses of a state of consciousness that can only be described as awareness, mindfulness or just witnessing. This is not a faraway realm, divorced from the everyday but is actually at the heart of it. Like a hole in the paper is both *in* the paper and yet not *of* paper, so is this state in the centre of the conscious self and yet beyond it.[2]

Consciousness, according to mystics, has two aspects—its contents and a 'knower' of these contents. Different schools have devised their own methods to perceive these two states. G.I. Gurdjieff, for example, taught in Paris during the first half of the twentieth century that we are all 'asleep', and to be 'awake' meant to be aware of the knower; unawareness of the knower amounted to being asleep.[3] This state of awakeness is made possible only by cultivating 'a continuous sense of "self-remembering" in the midst of everyday settings, where otherwise we lose ourselves and forget that we are alive'.[4] The Buddhists call this waking up mindfulness. Hindu Advaitic thought maintains that the conclusions drawn from the contents of consciousness (sense perceptions) are unreliable. To ascertain what is real we would have to step beyond the states of empirical existence and penetrate to the knower (pure consciousness).

My personal enquiry in this direction is grounded in my seven-year stay in Ashish's monastery. He believed consciousness can be known best only if you dig at one place—within yourself. And this, he emphasized, is done by observing yourself at all times, watching thoughts, watching yourself watching the thoughts. With the practise of watchfulness, the ubiquitous 'I' separates into an I that participates in experience and another I that observes the participation. The normal identification is with the participating 'I' but self-remembering initially helps to focus on the observer. This would make familiar an awareness[5] that participates in life, but through which you can also become aware of the knower.[6] The disciple's attempt is to rest in the knower. The journey then becomes a process of trying to 'awaken' to the knower; its discipline and practice an attempt to identify and weed out all that blocks the path.

In practising constant watchfulness, the dream-mirror can unravel the complexities of our emotional nature and reveal identifications that stand in the way of becoming aware. In these efforts meditation becomes the chief tool to identify the knower. It attempts to stop the internal chatter of thoughts—the contents of consciousness—in order to discover what lies beyond them. Fundamentally, the effort is to sit quietly and try by any means to stop the flow of thoughts. However, the attempt to quieten the mind throws up its own set of difficulties. Thoughts seem to have a life of their own. The attempt is not only to identify the personal compulsions that drive our thoughts during the short periods of meditation but also to practise being watchful all the time. Gradually, an awareness emerges which watches the play of thoughts and feelings, of joy and anger, rational and irrational arguments, of excuses, justifications, insincerities, of playing for attention, of feeling rejected—the whole gamut of positive and negative emotions.

According to Ashish, nothing is to be rejected; every experience is to be part of the effort towards self-awareness. Nothing will then be hidden, nothing feared or felt ashamed of. These aspects would need to be faced and integrated. A dream alerted me to this:

> *I'm telling the gardener that just watering the lawn is not enough. There are weeds which have to be pulled out too. I ardently advise him not to take care of only a part of the garden, but the whole of it.*

Ashish wrote, "The garden and lawn can represent the whole person, including the unconscious parts. You are the gardener. Taking care of the whole lawn and not just part of it implies that it is not enough to develop only particular qualities or abilities leaving the rest underdeveloped. The whole of you must be in harmony.

'Weeds in the dream could be mechanical thoughts, laziness, vague depressions, etc., which have to be uprooted, through meditation or otherwise.'

The way leads through yourself to beyond yourself.[7]

I also learnt about my own identifications through a dream when we were living in Ashish's ashram.

My mother and I are walking under her favourite umbrella. Unexpectedly, a large bird comes and takes away the umbrella. I am standing and laughing while my mother looks very crossly at the bird that can be seen in the sky carrying away the umbrella.

My sense of self was bound to my mother—I was walking under her umbrella. With the shift to the ashram I had physically moved away from her umbrella but I had not relinquished that identification internally. Symbolically, birds are often regarded as the vehicles by which we can rise out of ourselves. The discipline and practices of the ashram, perhaps, were the bird that could free me from my parental identifications, which, in turn, would help me stand back from myself. Till one is identified one is unable to separate the observer from the participant.

The next dream describes the beginning of this process of separation.

I am standing in the tea verandah and, from the window, I watch Persis in the garden, Michael going down to the dairy and Rajeev scrubbing the temple utensils outside the kitchen.

'Persis', 'Michael' and Rajeev were residents in the ashram and they perhaps represented various aspects of myself. Their activity, which I was viewing, was what constituted my workaday world. The dream was asking me to separate myself from my daily chores and dispassionately watch them. Actually, the tea verandah is a room on the first floor of the temple building where visitors met with Ashish over tea. Could the dream be punning on the word tea to signify teaching? In the evenings, after the day's work, we would meet there and discuss issues related to inner enquiry—essentially, how to withdraw from identifications and become the 'witness'.

While observing we tend to reflect on our thoughts and behaviour. This brings about a separation within us. But in this process, because the observer is identified with the personality, the observing part tends to evaluate the personality and wants to alter it.

However, if this identification were withdrawn then there would be sheer observation without any attempt to alter what is observed. This state of observation, free of identifications, is 'witnessing'. Ashish advised that this is not an intellectual trick where one is emotionally detached and views oneself as it were from behind one's eyes. Instead, a shift in identity is required.[8] Witnessing observes the mind while the mind is involved with thoughts and experiences. 'The child is after the toy, but the mother watches the child, not the toy.'[9]

Admittedly, the dream can also be viewed as an estrangement from my new environment. But then one would have to ask—which part of myself was disconnected from the everyday participative self? Either way, the dream is about the separation of awareness into an observer and a participant. In no way can this separation be confused for the fractured self because it is not a product of battling unconscious forces. Instead, it is the outcome of a voluntary process—a process familiar to and valued in all forms of psychotherapy. In the mystical journey it is considered the first step in turning inwards.

Gradually, this shift in outlook enlarged the scope of my dream life. A precognitive dream would occasionally burst through the haze of personality dreams. Sometimes a hint of guidance came my way. No longer was the dream only a personal mirror. At times the concerns of others also reflected telepathically in my dreams.

Ashish had gone from the ashram on a two-week-long trip, and was due to return on the sixteenth of that month. As the days passed we found ourselves looking forward to his return eagerly. I had a short dream:

> Our teacher has returned to the ashram on the fourteenth, two days before he was expected, and I am very surprised to see him.
>
> I say to him, 'But you were supposed to return on the sixteenth.'
>
> He does not answer but his lips betray a smile, possibly amused by my confusion. His eyes look straight at me as though searching for an explanation.

My surprise knew no bounds when he actually did return on the fourteenth, exactly as my dream had foretold! When asked about his early return, he replied matter-of-factly: 'The work finished earlier, so I came.' Then, as if in response to my surprise, he asked, 'Should I have stayed on?'

I was left bewildered. Had I been privy to a clue by which my subconscious mind had deduced that he would return earlier, and expressed it through the dream? If one such clue lies in past experience, then it went against my dream-dictated thesis because whenever our Teacher had left the ashram he would more often than not extend his trip due to delays in his work. Never had he come back earlier. I asked the other residents of the ashram whether they had entertained the possibility of his early return, but everyone had been surprised by his premature homecoming. If no subliminal hint had existed, then what was my dream? Precognition?

Other members of the ashram also had similar experiences. However exciting such experiences seemed, Ashish advised, 'If these paranormal dreams come, observe them, get used to them, read any message they may seem to give…and [move] on.'

I soon realized that some dreams now had a different *feel* to them. One evening, after a particularly strenuous day of manual labour on the farm, I had dozed off and I suddenly found myself out of my body, standing out in the open, looking at the night sky with its splash of stars. Then I drew back into my body as unexpectedly as I had left it. It was exhilarating to see the night sky without having left the room.

My elation was not at having exteriorized from the body; in fact, whether I had actually shed the body or not was unimportant. What was valuable was that this experience gave me a feel of what it is like to separate from the body. In doing so it provided a personal confirmation that awareness could exist apart from the body. The perception, I-am-not-only-the-body, grounded the practices within my experience. I also realized that this and similar dreams were not a consequence of my effort, my will. Humbly, I believed they were 'given' to me to affirm what I was seeking and to encourage my flailing attempts towards it.

The all-important lesson was that the attention has to be withdrawn from the identifications. Only then can we hope to quieten the mind. If we continue to watch the traffic in the street below our window, we will remain captivated. Only by withdrawing the attention can we become aware that the room we are standing in is actually a quiet one.

I was instructed in a dream to let the empirical personality die.

> *I am wandering around in a large empty haveli (mansion). A man appears in traditional Muslim attire. He is wearing a double-breasted swirling frock coat that comes below his knees. His name is Rumi. He takes me by the elbow and we go and sit outside the deserted haveli on the steps. In the fading evening light he says very softly, 'Die before thou diest...'*

I must describe my dream further. I saw a man twirling like the Dervishes and, when he faced me, I knew it was Rumi—Jalaluddin Rumi—the greatest mystical poet of Persia. A Jungian analyst would, of course, treat this dream as compensatory, and perhaps rightly so. During this phase my outer life in the ashram was most challenging—my identifications were under threat—and I was bolstering my sense of significance by dreaming about exalted people. The dream could equally be characterised as wish-fulfilment. However, these attributions do not exhaust all its significance. An entirely different meaning emerges if we consider 'die before thou diest' as the central message of the dream. I later discovered that this was a favourite phrase used by Rumi and attributed to the Prophet. Also,

Self-Enquiry and Dreams

this dying is not specific to Islam as it is echoed in the celebrated tribute to Saint Teresa of Avila:

> *Leave nothing of my Self in me;*
> *Let me so read thy life, that I*
> *Unto all life of mine may die.*

The axiom 'die before you die', is not about the small death of the body but the great death of the personality achieved by breaking all identifications with name and form (*nama-rupa*). According to Ashish, 'Then, when one goes in further [withdraws in meditation], it appears as if one was dying physically.'[10]

Stated differently, we can argue that the only certainty we possess is: I *am*. But we define ourselves as being 'this' or 'that'. We then convince ourselves that 'this' is mine. The withdrawal from these identifications, the relinquishing of 'this' or 'that' is the asked-for death. And strangely, the challenges in my outer life were pointing in the same direction. Since I was resisting them, the dream was, perhaps, asking me to make this surrender voluntarily.

The next dream is a hypnapompic one. Through the asleep–awake boundary, I clearly heard the words:

> *Find out what remains when you exhaust the content*
> *of all experience.*

Perhaps the key to the dream lies in the word *all*—all experience. It seemed to suggest that I had to empty myself of everything. Initially, my attempt on the journey had been to remove all the blocks and obstructions of the personality that could impede my search. Implicit in these attempts was the belief that only certain aspects had to be transformed. This dream was suggesting that all contents of experience, not only the blocks and difficulties but also the joy and contentment—in fact, all that constituted experience—had to be exhausted, dropped. I had to empty my mind of everything, leave behind all conceptions of myself and identify with nothing. Therefore, die before thou diest.

I still was unable to fathom where or to what this dying would lead? Whenever I meditated, whether in the morning or evening, the body and mind were already outwardly turned. I am not referring to the chatter of the mind, but to its instinctive out-turned orientation. Given this I had often reflected on how the silencing of thoughts or disregard of body-sensations is really possible.

I had a dream that seemed to reveal a level of consciousness which remains after the withdrawal of all identifications.

> *I am in an old Rajput fortress; the period is before our times. I am part of a rebellion to overthrow the existing King. I am standing in a room which is unoccupied, but the door is ajar and I can look into a large hall where many of the activities of the fort are taking place. There is a dancing woman in the hall with her red gauze and silver spangled skirt in full flare as she whirls around. Beyond the hall is the general bustle of the marketplace.*
>
> *Sita enters the room I am standing in and says with urgency that the rebellion, of which I was a part, had failed. She says, 'They have caught Pratap, your partner in the rebellion, and he's going to be beheaded tomorrow. They will capture you very soon and your*

death is inevitable. I don't want you to die in pain, so I will give you some sleeping pills. You just go to the other room, take them and slip out.' She clasps my hands and puts the sleeping pills into them. Then with a look of kindness she bids me farewell and leaves the room. I sit down on a chair and look towards the carnival of life from the half open door, knowing I am going to die soon. I don't seem to have any particular regrets about the whole thing.

I go into the adjoining room. It is very quiet. There is a bed in the centre of it and I realize I will not be disturbed here. It is the twilight hour. I draw the curtains in preparation. I sit on the bed, swallow the sleeping pills and lie down.

There was a dual quality to what happened next. In time I felt drowsy, but I was still aware of lying on the bed and of the room. Then, gradually, my breathing slowed down and the thought came to me: So, this is what dying is. After a little while my breath became almost imperceptible. Then a strange thing happened. I felt a sharp constriction in my chest; it was then released and I realized that I was sinking, lower and lower into a darkness that was in no way either frightening or uncomfortable. In fact, I stopped breathing. All that I remember was a slow and gradual stepping down into a vast darkness in which there was no object, no thought, no image, but only the sensation of sinking and perhaps a mild sensation of floating while sinking. The only thing that remained was an awareness of the experience. Yet it was not filtered through the person I normally know myself as. It was just an awareness that observed the experience.

Gradually, this awareness began to ascend and slowly I found myself coming back. With that came a dim recognition of my body lying prone on the bed, the eyes still closed, the curtains drawn, the twilight hour. And then the first thought came, 'Death or dhyan (meditative withdrawal)?'

The dream has two distinct parts. The events that lead to the taking of the sleeping pills, and the experience that ensues, which clearly was a form of dying. The image of a swirling garment perhaps links this dream to the previous one about the injunction to die before thou diest. Also, both the people in this dream are connected with Ashish. Sita is a friend associated with the ashram, while Pratap is a simple-minded local man who worked on the ashram farm when I lived there. I will explore the later part of the dream first, in which there is some measure of lucidity.

This part can be viewed as an imaginative rendering of the physical experience of dying—the drowsiness, slowing down of the breathing, the constriction in the chest could all have been based on memory, though I cannot identify any one specifically. Nor have I experienced a similar state during meditation. However, the strange part was that the *darkness* was not frightening or uncomfortable in any way. Had this experience been retrieved from the unconscious wouldn't there be resistance to it? And is there any kind of unconscious darkness with nothing in it, totally empty? Here there was just an impersonal awareness without any identifications—an observing state with nothing to observe. This awareness existed up to a point, after which there was submergence into an altogether different state, and subsequently (by implication) an arising out of it. It was not the state of quiescence that sometimes washes over one during meditation. The most prominent aspect of sinking into the darkness was the gradual withdrawal and then the complete absence of the normal waking state (or the dream state). There was no sense of a 'me' experiencing a descent, I found myself only after coming out of the darkness.

After regaining 'normal' consciousness within the dream arose the question: Was this an experience of death or of *dhyan*? Perhaps true *dhyan* is a dying, an annihilation of thoughts—the mind. The process of withdrawal from the sense organs in meditation (*dhyan*) is so similar to the withdrawal from the body at death that it appears like dying.[11] Was the dream a foretaste of the mystic death that Rumi had urged?

I must add that I am not prone to treating this dying as a process of psychotic disintegration, a relinquishing of the reality principle in favour of a regression to a narcissistically potent world. There was no world in this darkness, save only awareness. Urged by Sita, I had chosen the option of sleeping pills over that of beheading. It was, therefore, not an idiosyncratic and involuntary defence. This brings me to the first part of the dream.

Initially, I had regarded the earlier part of the dream as only a narrational container (Freud's visual representation) to get to the more important second part. However, later I was inclined to interpret it as having a close connection with the *dhyan*-dying part of the dream, perhaps hinting at the preparation required for true meditation (*dhyan*).

The symbols in the earlier part set the canvas of the dream's discourse. The King (the ego-personality or the waking integration) is entrenched in his fortress (of habits, beliefs, fixations). Commonly, the ego is considered sovereign when we explore consciousness, and is confused for the real 'I'. The rebellion is an attempt to rid the sovereignty of the ego (the King) and enquire: Who am I? But the dream cautions—a direct act of war cannot overthrow the waking integration from its position of dominance; the rebellion against the King will fail. In other words, I cannot enquire into consciousness in this simplistic manner (the simple-minded Pratap is my partner). The dream suggests that consciousness can only be explored by first withdrawing to an intermediate, unoccupied room, detached from the carnival of life (the large hall). The dancing woman represents not only sensuality but also the throb and dance of life. The door is not tightly shut but is ajar. Could this indicate that an isolated environment, a sequestered life, is not essential for this effort? I understood the twilight hour and the drawn curtains to mean that the intermediate room is a state in between waking and sleeping, when consciousness is neither awake nor asleep.

This left two options—getting beheaded or taking sleeping pills. Both are metaphors and both involve dying in some manner. I took the beheading to mean the quietening of the mind during meditation; the beheading of the waking mentation, as it were—thoughts, ideas and cognition. Could the sleeping pills be alluding to the state of sleep as another method to bypass the involvement with the King? Not the sleep of forgetfulness but an altogether different

Self-Enquiry and Dreams

kind of sleep wherein there is 'awakeness'. This is not the same as lucid dreaming but a state perhaps best described by Gackenbach's term 'witnessing dreaming' or 'witnessing sleep'.[12] A state of consciousness where the enthralment with waking life is absent and there is detachment from the dream state as well. The dream may be going on but the dreamer is aware of a calm, uninvolved luminous sense of awareness that observes the dream but is in no way identified with any part of it. As we saw in the previous chapter, some form of 'awakeness' has been found to be present in long-time meditators also in deep sleep.[13]

The difference between these two metaphors for dying is that 'beheading' is a method to explore consciousness in the waking state, while 'sleeping pills' refers to another way of continuing the exploration at night through sleep. 'It is a natural way in, followed by everyone every time sleep comes… That something stays awake, is a consequence of (a) the intention of staying awake and (b) the years of the practice of self-remembering which act to build the thing which does stay awake.'[14]

Was the dream stating that if I treat sleep and waking in the habitual (old fortress) manner, then the rebellion against the ego (the inner enquiry) would fail? Perhaps I need to behead my conception of what it means to be awake/asleep. Taking a dose of sleeping pills could imply putting to bed normal, conventional definitions—a reversal of normal conceptions, an inner awakeness while asleep and self-remembering while awake.

There was an unusual quality to this dreaming experience. Step by step I was taken from normal consciousness to a state beyond it where consciousness, without the content of experience, seemed to exist by itself. I was taken to the very frontiers of the known and made to face the immensity of the unknown. To dive deeper was up to me. Perhaps, to go deeper into this seeming darkness would depend upon my ability to let go of all identifications. And what lies beyond that darkness?

Much later, I had two other dreams, which appeared to address this whole issue from a different perspective. The first of these came against a background of emotional fatigue. Compounding this was an exceptionally hot Indian summer where repeated power cuts added to my discomfort. I emerged from sleep hearing the following words:

> *That comes to birth, That experiences and That goes out in death.*

What was left unsaid my thoughts completed as I came awake—'I' as the personality I knew myself to be had nothing to do with 'That'. It had certainly created a sharp division between the 'me' that considers itself the doer of all things and an impersonal 'I' that one is attempting to discover in meditation and by other practices. I took this dream as an affirmation of the message of the earlier one informing me about my inability to let go of the personal 'me'. The dream provided perspective by bluntly telling me: 'That' comes to birth, not you. Why? Because 'That' wishes to experience. It was in line with the Upanishadic message affirmed by mystics: 'That thou art'. What remains when everything else, every identification, is dropped cannot be 'me' but an impersonal 'That'. Another dream enlarged the perspective.

I had gone to sleep one afternoon when a noise from the direction of the roof jerked me 'awake'. I have no way of verifying whether there was actually a noise or whether it represented the jolt of becoming lucid. I was still enveloped by sleep but something was 'awake'.

Suddenly, consciousness, an impersonal awareness, rose from the depths of sleep. Quickly and rapidly it rose, till it came to the borders of wakefulness and then it attached itself to my personality. I first became aware of myself, and a split second later, my waking integration had taken over—cognizant of my surroundings, the room, the house.

When consciousness was rising from its depths it was 'nameless', without identity. I felt this was the same consciousness that had descended in the dream of death and *dhyan*. Here I experienced its ascent back into the known. I am not going to attempt any conceptual elaboration of this dream. Instead I quote two contemporary mystics.

Ramana Maharshi, the sage, says: 'In [deep] sleep there is no "I". The "I"-thought [the ego] arises on waking and then the world appears... At the time of waking up from sleep and before becoming aware of [the "I"-thought and] the world, there is that pure "I-I"... That subsists throughout. That is Consciousness. If that is known you will see that it is beyond thoughts.'[15] Anyone who had met Ramana believed the Maharshi constantly lived through this state of pure consciousness.

Nisargadatta Maharaj states: 'In reality there is only one state; when distorted by self-identification it is called a person, when coloured with the sense of being, it is the witness; when colourless and limitless, it is called the Supreme.'[16]

~

I had a dream a few days before a conference where I was due to present a paper. The dream seemed to span centuries and civilizations. Initially, I explored it as a reflection of my anxiety. But was there more to it than that? I believe so. This is how it went:

> *I see nomadic tribes, foraging for food, hunting, defending themselves. Then time moves on and I see Muslims, in black cloth headgears, swords in hand, mounted on horses, fighting over territory. The scene changes to the Nile where large stone blocks are being taken down the river in wooden boats for construction. Then somewhere near the coast of Greece a fleet of ships can be seen over the horizon.*
>
> *Throughout civilizations and centuries the debate remains the same—What is Reality? And this question is discussed animatedly on a podium that also looks like an amphitheatre. I am part of the debate and am wearing present-day clothes. People from earlier civilizations, like Greeks, Muslims and Romans are also there. I cannot remember the exact sequence of the debate, but it unfolded rather logically from one argument to the next.*
>
> *A Roman stood up and said, 'Reality is what we can create.'*
>
> *Another man said, 'Architecture is reality, new chariots and spears are reality.'*

Self-Enquiry and Dreams

> *A woman in a flowing robe stands up and pointing towards her heart says rather passionately, 'What you feel here is reality.'*
>
> *Each argument is discussed and commented upon. I listen and when there is a moment's pause I stand up and say, 'Ramana Maharshi's state of consciousness is Reality.'*
>
> *As soon as I finish many people rise in protest. A Greek says, 'That's intangible. It cannot be proved.'*
>
> *Another stands up and says, 'That's woolly stuff.' Someone thumps on the stone steps and says, 'A state of consciousness cannot be as real as physical objects. Sticks and stones are real, not what you are saying.'*
>
> *I am taken aback and realize that over the centuries the question of a state of consciousness like Ramana's being real has always been marginalized; rejected by the many, affirmed only by the very few. Yet my lone voice in that large crowd had produced a strong reaction. Then I realize that the crowd is waiting for me to say something more.*
>
> *I say, 'Your denial of this Reality is actually an affirmation of its existence.'*

As I awoke I wondered, 'Perhaps, there is only one Reality from which all other realities are born.'

Acknowledgements

To Sri Madhava Ashish for the gift of dream-work and for the ability to view dreams both as a mirror of the personality and as a gateway to transcendence.

To Ravi Singh for mooting the idea for this book with his special ability of giving an overview, of offering new perspectives, and for his insightful comments during its writing.

To Richa Singh for her engagement with dreams, for helping me connect with people some of whose dreams are there in the book, and for spearheading dream workshops. Her detailed and analytical comments on the draft of the book made me review aspects of it.

To Malashri Lal and Reba Som for their generosity in hosting dream discussions. To Alok Bhalla for the title of the book and to Six plus One for being able to share waking and sleeping dreams with.

To Shreya Gupta and Nazeef Mollah, my editors at Speaking Tiger, whose careful reading and comments helped enhance the book.

And specially to my A-team—Rajeev and Purnima—in continuing appreciation for their steadfast work on every book, as for this one too. Only team work makes the dream work!

Lastly, to the many people who shared a part of their lives with me. I can only hope I have done justice to their dreams.

Notes

1. Down the Rabbit Hole of Dreams
1. Caillois (1966), 34.
2. *Brahmavaivarta-Mahapurana*, vol. II (77.17), 502.

2. Oh! But Why Do We Dream?
1. Aserinsky and Kleitman were studying the sleeping behaviour of infants in their cribs, and were interested in observing the slow rolling of the eyes that accompanies sleep onset to determine whether they are related to the quality of sleep. They were unaware of the dream state being able to express itself as laboratory evidence.
2. Dement (1972), 28.

3. What's This Dream Telling Me?
1. To protect the privacy of people I have changed their names. Whenever this has been done, the first allusion to the name is enclosed in quotation marks.

4. Why Do We Keep Dreaming the Same Dreams?
1. See a brief biography of Calvin Hall (https://web.archive.org/web/20220328075606/www.dreams.ucsc.edu/About/calvin.html, last accessed July 25, 2022).
2. Castle (1994), 335.

3. 'How our dreams prepare us to face our fears', *ScienceDaily*, November 25, 2019 (https://www.sciencedaily.com/releases/2019/11/191125100349.htm, last accessed July 25, 2022).
4. Alpha rhythm is seen on the EEG and it often means that a person is focused on a specific thought and not paying attention to unwanted distractions. They tend to ignore sensory activity and are in a relaxed state. Alpha waves create a sense of peace and well-being in the mind and body.
5. Ullman and Zimmerman (1979), 102.
6. These are the findings of T. Benedek and B.B. Rubenstein which are reported in the *Psychosomatic Medicine Monographs*, nos. 1 & 2 for 1942. Quoted in Hall (1966), 241.
7. Hall (1966), 49.
8. Fontana (1994), 75.
9. Hazarika (1997), 135.
10. Freud (1900), 277–79.
11. Young (199), 48–49.
12. *Brahamavaivarta-Mahapuranam*, vol. II, 522.
13. Lorand, quoted in Delaney (1991), 360.
14. Delaney (1991), 361.
15. Castle (1994), 339.
16. Freud (1900), 422n1.
17. Castle (1994), 340–41.
18. Bettelheim (1975), 18.
19. Ibid., 6.
20. Castle (1994), 341.
21. Jung (1964), 40.

5. Nightmares: Terrors of the Dreaming World

1. Galvin and Hartmann (1999), 236.
2. Hartmann (1996), 111–13.

3. Galvin and Hartmann (1999), 239.
4. Delaney (1991), 358.
5. Castle (1994), 347.
6. Ibid.
7. Hartmann, 107.
8. Ibid., 100.
9. Ibid., 109.

9. The Snake Catches Its Tail: Breakthrough Dreams

1. Kaempffert (1924), 385. Quoted in LaBerge (1986), 187–88.
2. Castle (1994), 36.
3. Stevens (1996), 283.
4. Gandhi (1927), 348.
5. Ullman et al. (1973), 178.
6. Stevens (1996), 283.
7. Bryson (2004), 184–87.
8. Koestler (1964), 118.
9. Ibid., 146.
10. Loewi (1960), as quoted in Edwin Diamond, *The Science of Dreams* (New York: MacFadden Books, 1963), 155. Quoted in Garfield (1995), 68–69.
11. Stevens (1996), 285.
12. Koestler (1964), 116–17.
13. Kedrov, quoted in LaBerge (1986), 187.
14. Stevenson, 'A Chapter on Dreams', 172. Quoted in Garfield (1995), 71, and in Woods and Greenhouse (1974), 55–56.
15. Ibid., 167, quoted in Garfield (1995), 70.
16. Ibid., 171, quoted in Garfield (1995), 71.
17. Gaskell, 'The Life of Charlotte Bronte', quoted in Ratcliff (1996), 88–89.
18. Garfield (1995), 64.
19. Kinder (1988), 186, quoted in Castle (1994), 12.
20. Dement (1972), 101

10. The Sentinels of the Body—Illness and Healing Dreams

1. Mitchell, quoted in Castle (1994), 368.
2. Lockhart (1977), quoted in Castle (1994), 36.
3. Siegel, quoted in Castle (1994), 366.
4. *The Parisistas of the Atharvaveda* (68.1.51), quoted in O'Flaherty (1984), 19.
5. *Susruta Samhita* (I.29.68), quoted in O'Flaherty (1984), 23.
6. Potter (1977), 293–94, quoted in O'Flaherty (1984), 25.
7. Master (1999).
8. Garfield (1991), 69.

11. Seriously Strange: The Paranormal Dream

1. Franz (1966), quoted in Ullman (1973), 27.
2. *The Parisistas of the Atharvaveda* (68.2.57–59); *Agni Purana* (229.16–19); *Matsya Purana* (242.16–20); *Brahmavaivarta Mahapuranam* (*Krsna-Janma Khanda*) (77.4–8). The period in which the outcome fructifies varies slightly between texts.
3. *Mysteries of the Unknown*, 29.
4. Ibid.
5. Barker, quoted in Castle (1994), 408.
6. Dunne (1927), 53.
7. Hill (1967), 30, quoted in Ullman et al. (1973), 6.
8. *Mysteries of the Unknown*, 50–53 and 69.
9. Ullman et al. (1973), 148–49.
10. Tabori, quoted in Ullman et al. (1973), 25.

12. Dying and Mourning

1. Garfield (1996), 187.
2. Ibid., 201.
3. Garfield (1996), 198.

4. Homer, *Iliad*, Book XXIII, 315–16.
5. Fourtier (1972), 1, quoted in Bulkeley (1994), 163.

13. Awake and Dreaming—The Lucid Dream

1. Green (1968), 160, quoted in Hunt (1989), 119.
2. Moffit et al. (1986).
3. LaBerge (1986), 85–86.
4. Ibid., 87–88.
5. Ibid., 82.
6. Ibid., 95.
7. Moffit et al. (1986).
8. Castle (1994), 52.
9. Ibid., 39.
10. Ibid., 39–41.
11. Sviri (1999), 259.
12. Bulkeley (1999), 211.
13. Underhill (1911), 279.
14. Alexander et al. (1985).
15. Ouspensky (1950), 147.
16. Gackenbach (1997), 109.
17. Alexander et al. (1985).
18. Gackenbach (1997), 108.
19. Quoted in Gackenbach (1988).

14. Self-Enquiry and Dreams: Dreaming in a Himalayan Monastery

1. A large part of this article was published in the anthology *On Dreams and Dreaming*, edited by Sudhir Kakar (New Delhi: Penguin, 2011), 146–67. It was the outcome of a symposium held at Wasan Island in Lake Muskoka in Ontario, Canada on the 'Boundaries of Consciousness'.
2. Nisargadatta Maharaj (1973), 34.
3. Ouspensky (1950), 141–45.

4. Hunt (1986).
5. 'The vocabulary for this subject has not been fully worked out...and one tends to get bogged down in clashing jargons of different schools. I find it useful to use "consciousness" to refer to all the processes concerned with sensing (seeing, hearing, etc.) and the conversion of electromagnetic waves into mental images. I prefer to restrict awareness to the faculty/power which *observes* the images/thoughts/feelings. Awareness does not think: it observes the thinking process. It does not concentrate: it observes the concentration of attention. This is why it usually has to be found/identified first in a meditation practice which aims at *stopping* all perception of sensation, thought, etc. When the operations of the mind are stopped, then what is left is awareness.' Sri Madhava Ashish (1998), 30.
6. 'Consciousness is like a light which, while revealing objects, also reveals itself; when it throws light on objects around it, it is capable of illuminating itself.' See Santokh Singh, *Consciousness as Ultimate Principle* (New Delhi: Munshiram Manoharlal Publishers, 1985), 3.
7. Nisargadatta Maharaj Op. cit., 166
8. Ashish (1998), 26. 'What occurs during meditative contemplation in a tradition such as Buddhism and what occurs during introspection in the ordinary sense are two different things.' See H.H. the Dalai Lama, *The Universe in a Single Atom* (London: Little, Brown, 2006), 145.
9. Nisargadatta Maharaj (1973), 221.
10. Ashish (1998), 13.
11. Ibid., 50.
12. Gackenbach (1997).
13. Alexander et al. (1985).
14. Ashish (1998), 26–27.
15. Sri Ramana Maharshi (1998), 99–100.
16. Nisargadatta Maharaj (1973), 401.

Select Bibliography

Agni Puranam, 2 Vols. 1967. Translated by Manmatha Nath Dutt Shastri. Varanasi: Chowkhamba Sanskrit Series.

Alexander, C.N., R. Boyer, and D. Orme-Johnson. 1985. 'Distinguishing between transcendental consciousness and lucidity'. *Lucidity Letter* 4(2): 68–85.

Ashish, Sri Madhava. 1998. Untitled collection of extracts of letters. Compiled by John Donovan. Unpublished manuscript.

Barker, J. 1967. 'Premonitions of the Aberfan Disaster'. *Journal of the Society for Psychical Research* 44: 169–81.

Bettelheim, Bruno. (1975) 1991. *The Uses of Enchantment: The Meaning and Importance of Fairy Tales*. London: Penguin.

Brahmavaivarta Mahapuranam, 2 Vols. 2001. Translated by Shanti Lal Nagar. Delhi: Parimal Publications.

Bryson, Bill. 2004. *A Short History of Nearly Everything*. London: Black Swan.

Bulkeley, Kelly. 1994. *The Wilderness of Dreams: Exploring the Religious Meanings of Dreams in Modern Western Culture*. Albany: State University of New York Press.

_____.1999. 'The Interpretation of Spiritual Dreams throughout History'. In Krippner and Waldman (eds.), *Dreamscaping*, 198–220.

Caillois, Roger. 1966. 'Logical and Philosophical Problems of the Dream'. In Grunebaum and Caillois (eds.), *The Dream and Human Societies*, 23–52.

Castle, Robert L. Van de. 1994. *Our Dreaming Mind*. New York: Aquarian.

Delaney, Gayle. 1991. *Breakthrough Dreaming*. New York: Bantam.

Dement, William C. 1972. *Some Must Watch While Some Must Sleep*. Stanford, California: Stanford Alumni Association.

Dunne, J.W. (1927) 1964. *An Experiment with Time*. London: Faber and Faber.

Fontana, David. 1994. *The Secret Language of Dreams*. Rev. ed. London: Piatkus, 1997.

Fourtier, Millie Kelly. 1972. *Dreams and Preparation for Death*. Ann Arbor, Mich.: University Microfilms.

Franz, M.L. von. 1966. 'Time and Synchronicity in Analytical Psychology'. In *The Voices of Time*, edited by J.T. Fraser. New York: Brazillier.

Freud, S. (1900) 1965. *The Interpretation of Dreams*. Translated by James Strachey. New York: Avon Books.

Gackenbach, J. 1988. 'From Sleep Consciousness to Pure Consciousness'. Presidential address to the annual meeting of the Association for the Study of Dreams, London (https://academic.macewan.ca/gackenbachj/unpublished-papers/higher-states-of-consciousness/from-sleep-consciousness-to-pure-consciousness/, last accessed July 25, 2022).

_____.1997. 'Lucid Dreaming'. In Varela (ed.), *Sleeping, Dreaming and Dying*, 101–10.

_____,W. Moorecroft, C. Alexander, and S. LaBerge. 1987. 'Physiological correlates of "consciousness" during sleep in a single TM practitioner'. *Sleep Research* 16: 230.

Galvin, Franklin, and Ernest Hartmann. 1999. 'Nightmares: Terrors of the Dreaming World'. In Krippner and Waldman (eds.), *Dreamscaping*, 236–44.

Gandhi, M.K. (1927) 1972. *The Story of My Experiments with Truth*. Ahmedabad: Navajivan Publishing House.

Garfield, Patricia. 1991. *The Healing Power of Dreams*. New York: Simon and Schuster.

———.1995. *Creative Dreaming*. New York: Fireside Book.

———.1996. 'Dreams in Bereavement'. In *Trauma and Dreams*, edited by D. Barrett (Cambridge, MA: Harvard University Press), 186–211.

Green, Celia. 1968. *Lucid Dreams*. New York: Hamish Hamilton.

Grunebaum, G.E. von, and R. Caillois, eds. 1966. *The Dream and Human Societies*. Berkeley: University of California Press.

Hall, C.S. 1966. *The Meaning of Dreams*. New York: McGraw-Hill. First published in 1953.

Hartmann, Earnest. 1996. 'Who Develops PTSD Nightmares and Who Doesn't'. In Barrett (ed.), *Trauma and Dreams*, 100–13.

Hazarika, Anjali. 1997. *Daring to Dream: Cultivating Corporate Creativity Through Dreamwork*. New Delhi: Response Books.

Hill, R., ed. 1967. *Such Stuff as Dreams*. London: R. Hart-Davis.

Homer. *The Iliad*. Ware, Hertfordshire: Wordsworth Classics, 1995.

Hunt, Harry T. 1986. 'Lucid Dreams & Meditation'. *Lucidity Letter* 5(1): 31–37.

———.1989. *The Multiplicity of Dreams: Memory, Imagination and Consciousness*. New Haven: Yale University Press.

Jung, C.G. 1964. 'Approaching the Unconscious'. In *Man and His Symbols*, edited by Carl Jung (London: Picador, 1978).

Kaempffert, W. 1924. *A Popular History of American Invention*, Vol II. New York: Charles Scribner's Sons.

Kasatkin, V.N. 1967. *Teoria Snovidenni* [Theory of Dreams]. Leningrad: Meditsina.

Kedrov, B.M. 1957. 'On the question of Scientific Creativity'. *Voprosy Psikologii* 3: 91–113.

Kinder, M. 1988. 'The Dialectic of Dreams and Theater in the Films of Ingmar Bergman'. *Dreamworks* 5(3/4): 179–92.

Koestler, Arthur. 1964. *The Act of Creation*. London: Hutchinson. (Repr. London: Arkana, 1989.)

Krippner, Stanley, and M.R. Waldman, eds. 1999. *Dreamscaping: New and Creative Ways to Work with Your Dreams*. Los Angeles: Roxbury Park.

LaBerge, Stephen. 1986. *Lucid Dreaming*. New York: Ballantine Books.

Lockhart, R.A. 1977. 'Cancer in Myth and Dream: An Exploration into the Archetypal Relation Between Dreams and Disease'. *Spring* 1: 1–26.

Loewi, Otto. 1960. 'An Autobiographic Sketch'. *Perspectives in Biology and Medicine*, Autumn.

Lorand, S. 1957. 'Dream Interpretation in the Talmud'. *The International Journal of Psycho-Analysis* 38: 95.

Master, F.J. 1999. *Dictionary of the Dreams in Homoeopathy*. New Delhi: B. Jain Publishers.

The Matsya Puranam. Translated by S.C. Vasu and edited by J.D. Akhtar. Delhi: Oriental Publishers, 1972.

Mitchell, E. 1923. 'The Physiological Diagnostic Dream'. *New York Medical Journal* 118: 417.

Moffit, Alan, S. Purcell, R. Hoffman, R. Pigeau, and R. Wells. 1986. 'Dream psychology: Operating in the dark'. *Lucidity Letter* 5(1): 180–96.

Mysteries of the Unknown: Psychic Powers. Alexandria, Virginia: Time-Life Books, 1995.

Nisargadatta Maharaj, Sri. (1973) 1997. *I am That*. Translated by Maurice Frydman. Bombay: Chetana.

O'Flaherty, Wendy Doniger, ed. 1983. *Karma and Rebirth in Classical Indian Traditions*. Delhi: Motilal Banarsidass Publishers.

_____.1984. *Dreams, Illusion, and Other Realities*. Chicago: University of Chicago Press.

Ouspensky, P.D. 1950. *In Search of the Miraculous*. London: Routledge & Kegan Paul.

The Parisistas of the Atharvaveda. (1909) 1976. Edited by G.M. Bolling and J. von Negelein. Hindi notes by R.K. Rai. Varanasi: Chaukhambha Orientalia.

Potter, Karl H. 1977. *Indian Metaphysics and Epistemology: The Tradition of Nyaya-Vaisesika up to Gangesa*. Princeton: Princeton University Press.

Ramana Maharshi, Sri. 1998. *Conscious Immortality: Conversations with Sri Ramana Maharshi*. Recorded by Paul Brunton & Mungala Venkataramiah. Tiruvannamalai, Tamil Nadu: Sri Ramanasramam.

Ratcliff, A.J.J. 1996. *A History of Dreams*. London: Senate.

Shulman, David, and Guy G. Stroumsa, eds. 1999. *Dream Cultures: Explorations in the Comparative History of Dreaming*. New York: Oxford University Press.

Siegel, B. 1989. *Peace, Love and Healing*. New York: Harper & Row.

Stevens, Anthony. 1996. *Private Myths: Dreams and Dreaming*. London: Penguin Books. First published in 1995.

Stevenson, R.L. 1925. *Memories and Portraits, Random Memories of Himself*. New York: Scribner.

Susruta Samhita. 1980. Translated by P. Ray, H. Gupta and Mira Roy. New Delhi: Indian National Science Academy.

Sviri, Sara. 1999. 'Dreaming Analyzed and Recorded: Dreams in the World of Medieval Islam'. In Shulman and Stroumsa (eds.), *Dream Cultures*, 252–73.

Tabori, C. 1951. *My Occult Diary*. Quoted in *They Knew the Unknown* by M. Ebon (New York: World, 1971).

Ullman, M., Stanley Krippner, and Alan Vaughan. 1973. *Dream Telepathy: Experiments in Nocturnal Extrasensory*

Perception. Charlottesville, Virginia: Hampton Roads Publishing Co., 2002.

———, and N. Zimmerman. 1979. *Working with Dreams.* New York: Tarcher/Putnam.

Underhill, Evelyn. (1911) 1999. *Mysticism: The Nature and Development of Spiritual Consciousness.* Oxford: Oneworld.

Varela, F.J., ed., and narrator. 1997. *Sleeping, Dreaming and Dying: An Exploration of Consciousness with The Dalai Lama.* Boston: Wisdom Publications.

Woods, R.L., and H.B. Greenhouse, eds. 1974. *The New World of Dreams.* New York: Macmillan Publishing Co.

Young, Serinity. 1999. *Dreaming in the Lotus: Buddhist Dream Narrative, Imagery, and Practice.* Boston: Wisdom Publications.